D1376283

the complete
Come and Praise
WORDS EDITION

Compiled by Geoffrey Marshall-Taylor
Arrangements by Douglas Coombes

BBC

Contents

Praise and thanksgiving

The journey of life

Songs of worship

Easter

Harvest

Peace

1

1 Morning has broken,
Like the first morning,
Blackbird has spoken
Like the first bird.
Praise for the singing!
Praise for the morning!
Praise for them, springing
Fresh from the Word!

2 Sweet the rain's new fall
Sunlit from heaven,
Like the first dewfall
On the first grass.
Praise for the sweetness
Of the wet garden,
Sprung in completeness
Where his feet pass.

3 Mine is the sunlight!
Mine is the morning
Born of the one light
Eden saw play!
Praise with elation,
Praise every morning,
God's re-creation
Of the new day!
Eleanor Farjeon

2

1 Have you heard the raindrops drumming on the
roof-tops?
Have you heard the raindrops dripping on the
ground?
Have you heard the raindrops splashing in the
streams and running to the rivers all around?

Chorus:
There's water, water of life,
Jesus gives us the water of life;
There's water, water of life,
Jesus gives us the water of life.

2 There's a busy workman digging in the desert,
Digging with a spade that flashes in the sun;
Soon there will be water rising in the wellshaft,
spilling from the bucket as it comes.
Chorus

3 Nobody can live who hasn't any water,
When the land is dry then nothing much grows;
Jesus gives us life if we drink the living water,
sing it so that everybody knows.
Chorus

Christian Strover

3

Chorus:
All things bright and beautiful,
All creatures great and small,
All things wise and wonderful,
The Lord God made them all.

1 Each little flower that opens,
Each little bird that sings,
He made their glowing colours,
He made their tiny wings:
Chorus

2 The purple-headed mountain,
The river running by,
The sunset and the morning,
That brightens up the sky:
Chorus

3 The cold wind in the winter,
The pleasant summer sun,
The ripe fruits in the garden,
He made them every one:
Chorus

4 He gave us eyes to see them,
And lips that we might tell
How great is God Almighty,
Who has made all things well:
Chorus

Cecil Frances Alexander

4

1 Autumn days when the grass is jewelled
And the silk inside a chestnut shell,
Jet planes meeting in the air to be refuelled,
All these things I love so well.

Chorus:
So I mustn't forget.
No, I mustn't forget,
To say a great big thank-you,
I mustn't forget.

2 Clouds that look like familiar faces,
And a winter's moon with frosted rings,
Smell of bacon as I fasten up my laces,
And the song the milkman sings.
Chorus

3 Whipped-up spray that is rainbow-scattered,
And a swallow curving in the sky.
Shoes so comfy though they're worn-out and
they're battered,
And the taste of apple-pie.
Chorus

4 Scent of gardens when the rain's been falling,
And a minnow darting down a stream,
Picked-up engine that's been stuttering and
stalling,
And a win for my home team.
Chorus

Estelle White

5

1 Carpenter, carpenter, make me a tree,
That's the work of somebody far greater
than me;
Gardener, gardener, shape me a flower,
That's the work of somebody with far greater
power.

Chorus:
Somebody greater than you or me,
Put the apple on the apple tree;
The flower in the earth and the fish in the sea,
Are by somebody greater than you or me.

2 Builder, now raise up a coloured rainbow,
That's something far greater than people could know;
Farmer, I ask you, design me some corn,
That's somebody greater than any man born.
Chorus

3 Now, electrician, will you light a star,
That's the work of somebody who's greater by far;
Plumber, connect up the river and sea,
That's the work of somebody far greater than me.
Chorus

Marion Payton

6

1 The earth is yours, O God,
You nourish it with rain;
The streams and rivers overflow,
The land bears seeds again.

2 The soil is yours, O God,
The shoots are moist with dew,
And, ripened by the burning sun,
The corn grows straight and true.

3 The hills are yours, O God,
Their grass is lush and green,
Providing pastures for the flocks,
Which everywhere are seen.

4 The whole rich land is yours,
For fodder or for plough,
And so, for rain, sun, soil and seed,
O God, we thank you now.

Michael Saward

7

1 All creatures of our God and King,
Lift up your voice and with us sing,
Alleluia, Alleluia!
You burning sun with golden beam,
You silver moon with softer gleam,

Chorus:
O praise Him, O praise Him,
Alleluia, Alleluia, Alleluia!

2 You rushing wind who are so strong,
You clouds that sail in heaven along,
O praise Him, Alleluia!
You rising morn, in praise rejoice,
You lights of evening, find a voice.
Chorus

3 You flowing water, pure and clear,
Make music for your Lord to hear,
Alleluia, Alleluia!
You fire so masterful and bright,
Who gives to man both warmth and light,
Chorus

4 Let all things their Creator bless,
And worship Him in humbleness,
O praise Him, Alleluia!
Praise, praise the Father, praise the Son,
And praise the Spirit, Three in One.
Chorus

Words: William Draper Tune: Lasst uns erfreuen

8

1 Let us with a gladsome mind
Praise the Lord, for He is kind:

Chorus:
For His mercies still endure,
Ever faithful, ever sure.

2 Let us blaze His name abroad,
For of gods He is the God:
Chorus

3 He, with all-commanding might,
   Filled the new-made world with light:
   Chorus

4 All things living He does feed,
   His full hand supplies their need:
   Chorus

5 Let us with gladsome mind
   Praise the Lord, for He is kind:
   Chorus

                              John Milton

9

1 Fill your hearts with joy and gladness,
   Sing and praise your God and mine!
   Great the Lord in love and wisdom,
   Might and majesty divine!
   He who framed the starry heavens
   Knows and names them as they shine.

2 Praise the Lord for times and seasons,
   Cloud and sunshine, wind and rain;
   Spring to melt the snows of winter
   Till the waters flow again;
   Grass upon the mountain pastures,
   Golden valleys thick with grain.

3 Fill your hearts with joy and gladness,
   Peace and plenty crown your days;
   Love His laws, declare His judgements,
   Walk in all His words and ways,
   He the Lord and we His children;
   Praise the Lord, all people, praise!
                      Timothy Dudley-Smith

   • *Repeat the last line of each verse for Tune 2.*

10

1 God who made the earth,
   The air, the sky, the sea,
   Who gave the light its birth,
   Careth for me.

2 God who made the grass,
The flower, the fruit, the tree,
The day and night to pass,
Careth for me.

3 God who made the sun,
The moon, the stars, is He
Who, when life's clouds come on,
Careth for me.
Sarah Rhodes

11

1 For the beauty of the earth,
For the beauty of the skies,
For the love which from our birth
Over and around us lies,
Father, unto Thee we raise
This our sacrifice of praise.

2 For the beauty of each hour
Of the day and of the night,
Hill and vale and tree and flower,
Sun and moon and stars of light,
Father, unto Thee we raise
This our sacrifice of praise.

3 For the joy of human love,
Brother, sister, parent, child,
Friends on earth and friends above,
For all gentle thoughts and mild,
Father, unto Thee we raise
This our sacrifice of praise.

4 For each perfect gift of Thine
To our race so freely given,
Graces human and divine,
Flowers of earth and buds of heaven,
Father, unto Thee we raise
This our sacrifice of praise.
Folliott Pierpoint

12

1 Who put the colours in the rainbow?
Who put the salt into the sea?
Who put the cold into the snowflake?
Who made you and me?
Who put the hump upon the camel?
Who put the neck on the giraffe?
Who put the tail upon the monkey?
Who made hyenas laugh?
  Who made whales and snails and quails?
  Who made hogs and dogs and frogs?
  Who made bats and rats and cats?
  Who made everything?

2 Who put the gold into the sunshine?
Who put the sparkle in the stars?
Who put the silver in the moonlight?
Who made Earth and Mars?
Who put the scent into the roses?
Who taught the honey bee to dance?
Who put the tree inside the acorn?
It surely can't be chance!
  Who made seas and leaves and trees?
  Who made snow and winds that blow?
  Who made streams and rivers flow?
  God made all of these!

Paul Booth

13

1 Oh praise Him!
Oh praise Him!
Oh praise Him!
Oh praise Him!
Oh praise Him!
Oh praise Him!
He made the heavens, He made our sky,
The sun, the moon, the stars on high.
He formed our world, His mighty hand
Divided sea and land.
He moves in wind and rain and snow,
His life is in all things that grow.
Oh praise Him!
Oh praise Him!
Oh praise Him!

2 Oh praise Him!
  Oh praise Him!
  Oh praise Him!
  Oh praise Him!
  Oh praise Him!
  Oh praise Him!
  His joy is in the eagle's flight,
  The tiger's roar, the lion's might
  The lamb, the python and the whale,
  The spider, ant and snail.
  All things that leap and swim and fly
  On land and sea and in the sky,
  They praise Him,
  They praise Him,
  They praise Him.

3 Oh praise Him!
  Oh praise Him!
  Oh praise Him!
  Oh praise Him!
  Oh praise Him!
  Oh praise Him!
  He lives His life in love and joy
  In man and woman, girl and boy.
  His purpose is in me and you,
  In what we are and do.
  His love is in us when we sing
  With every God-created thing,
  And praise Him,
  And praise Him,
  And praise Him.

Arthur Scholey

14

Chorus:
All the nations of the earth,
Praise the Lord who brings to birth
The greatest star, the smallest flower:
Alleluia.

1 Let the heavens praise the Lord:
Alleluia.
Moon and stars, praise the Lord:
Alleluia.
Chorus

2 Snow-capped mountains, praise the Lord:
Alleluia.
Moon and stars, praise the Lord:
Alleluia.
Chorus

3 Deep sea-water, praise the Lord:
Alleluia.
Gentle rain, praise the Lord:
Alleluia.
Chorus

4 Roaring lion, praise the Lord:
Alleluia.
Singing birds, praise the Lord:
Alleluia.
Chorus

5 Kings and princes, praise the Lord:
Alleluia.
Young and old, praise the Lord:
Alleluia.
Chorus

Michael Cockett

15

1 There are hundreds of sparrows, thousands,
millions,
They're two a penny, far too many there
must be;
There are hundreds and thousands,
millions of sparrows,
But God knows every-one and God knows me.

2 There are hundreds of flowers, thousands,
millions,
And flowers fair the meadows wear for all
to see;
There are hundreds and thousands,
millions of flowers,
But God knows every-one and God knows me.

3 There are hundreds of planets, thousands,
millions,
Way out in space each has a place by
God's decree;
There are hundreds and thousands,
millions of planets,
But God knows every-one and God knows me.

4 There are hundreds of children, thousands,
millions,
And yet their names are written on
God's memory,
There are hundreds and thousands,
millions of children,
But God knows every-one and God knows me!

John Gowans

16

1 When God made the garden of creation,
He filled it full of His love;
When God made the garden of creation,
He saw that it was good.
There's room for you,
And room for me,
And room for everyone:
For God is a Father, who loves His children,
And gives them a place in the sun.
When God made the garden of creation,
He filled it full of His love.

2 When God made the hamper of creation,
He filled it full of His love;
When God made the hamper of creation,
He saw that it was good.
There's food for you,
And food for me,
And food for everyone:
But man is so greedy and wastes God's bounty,
That some won't get any at all.
When God made the hamper of creation,
He filled it full of His love.

3 When God made the family of creation,
He made it out of His love;
When God made the family of creation,
He saw that it was good.
There's love for you,
And love for me,
And love for everyone:
But man is so selfish, ignores his neighbour,
And seeks his own place in the sun.
When God made the family of creation,
He made it out of His love.

4 When God made the garden of creation,
He filled it full of His love;
When God made the garden of creation,
He saw that it was good.
There's room for you,
And room for me,
And room for everyone:

For God is a Father, who loves His children,
And gives them a place in the sun.
When God made the garden of creation,
He filled it full of His love.

Paul Booth

17

1 Think of a world without any flowers,
Think of a world without any trees,
Think of a sky without any sunshine,
Think of the air without any breeze.
We thank you, Lord, for flowers and trees and
sunshine,
We thank you, Lord, and praise your holy
name.

2 Think of a world without any animals,
Think of a field without any herd,
Think of a stream without any fishes,
Think of a dawn without any bird.
We thank you, Lord, for all your living
creatures,
We thank you, Lord, and praise your holy
name.

3 Think of a world without any people,
Think of a street with no-one living there,
Think of a town without any houses,
No-one to love and nobody to care.
We thank you, Lord, for families and
friendships,
We thank you, Lord, and praise your holy
name.

Doreen Newport

18

1 He gave me eyes so I could see
The wonders of the world;
Without my eyes I could not see
The other boys and girls.
He gave me ears so I could hear
The wind and rain and sea.
I've got to tell it to the world,
He made me.

2 He gave me lips so I could speak
And say what's in my mind;
Without my lips I could not speak
A single word or line.
He made my mind so I could think,
And choose what I should be.
I've got to tell it to the world,
He made me.

3 He gave me hands so I could touch,
And hold a thousand things;
I need my hands to help me write,
To help me fetch and bring.
These feet He made so I could run,
He meant me to be free.
I've got to tell it to the world,
He made me.

Alan Pinnock

19

Chorus:
He's got the whole world, in His hand,
He's got the whole wide world, in His hand,
He's got the whole world, in His hand,
He's got the whole world in His hand.

1 He's got the wind and the rain, in His hand,
He's got the wind and the rain, in His hand,
He's got the wind and the rain, in His hand,
He's got the whole world in His hand.
Chorus

2 He's got the sun and the moon, in His hand,
   He's got the sun and the moon, in His hand,
   He's got the sun and the moon, in His hand,
   He's got the whole world in His hand.
   Chorus

3 He's got the plants and the creatures,
   in His hand,
   He's got the plants and the creatures,
   in His hand,
   He's got the plants and the creatures,
   in His hand,
   He's got the whole world in His hand.
   Chorus

4 He's got everybody here, in His hand,
   He's got everybody here, in His hand,
   He's got everybody here, in His hand,
   He's got the whole world in His hand.
   Chorus

Traditional

20

1 Come, my brothers, praise the Lord, alleluia.
   He's our God and we are His, alleluia.

2 Come to Him with songs of praise, alleluia.
   Songs of praise, rejoice in Him, alleluia.

3 For the Lord is a mighty God, alleluia.
   He is King of all the world, alleluia.

4 In His hands are valleys deep, alleluia.
   In His hands are mountain peaks, alleluia.

5 In His hands are all the seas, alleluia.
   And the lands which He has made, alleluia.

6 Come, my brothers, praise the Lord, alleluia.
   He's our God and we are His, alleluia.

Traditional

21

Chorus:
Come and praise the Lord our King, Hallelujah,
Come and praise the Lord our King, Hallelujah.

1 Christ was born in Bethlehem, Hallelujah,
  Son of God and Son of Man, Hallelujah.
  Chorus

2 From him love and wisdom came, Hallelujah;
  All his life was free from blame, Hallelujah.
  Chorus

3 Jesus died at Calvary, Hallelujah,
  Rose again triumphantly, Hallelujah.
  Chorus

4 He will be with us today, Hallelujah,
  And forever with us stay, Hallelujah.
  Chorus

Traditional (adapted)

22

1 I danced in the morning
  When the world was begun,
  And I danced in the moon
  And the stars and the sun;
  And I came down from heaven
  And I danced on the earth;
  At Bethlehem
  I had my birth.

Chorus:
Dance then, wherever you may be,
I am the Lord of the Dance, said he,
And I'll lead you all wherever you may be,
And I'll lead you all in the dance, said he.

2 I danced for the scribe
  And the pharisee,
  But they would not dance
  And they wouldn't follow me.

I danced for the fishermen,
For James and John —
They came with me
And the dance went on.
Chorus

3 I danced on the Sabbath
And I cured the lame;
The holy people
Said it was a shame.
They whipped and they stripped
And they hung me on high,
And they left me there
On a cross to die.
Chorus

4 They cut me down
And I leapt up high;
I am the life
That'll never, never die.
I'll live in you
If you live in me;
I am the Lord
Of the Dance, said he.
Chorus

Sydney Carter

23

1 Jesus, good above all other,
Gentle child of gentle mother,
In a stable born our brother,
Give us grace to persevere.

2 Jesus, cradled in a manger,
For us facing every danger,
Living as a homeless stranger,
We make you our King most dear.

3 Jesus, for your people dying,
Risen Master, death defying,
Lord in heaven, your grace supplying,
Keep us to your presence near.

4 Lord, in all our doings guide us,
  Pride and hate shall ne'er divide us,
  We'll go on with you beside us,
  And with joy we'll persevere!

Percy Dearmer

24

Chorus:
Go, tell it on the mountain,
Over the hills and everywhere;
Go, tell it on the mountain
That Jesus is his name.

1 He possessed no riches, no home to lay his head;
  He saw the needs of others and cared for them
  instead.
  Chorus

2 He reached out and touched them, the blind,
  the deaf, the lame;
  He spoke and listened gladly to anyone
  who came.
  Chorus

3 Some turned away in anger, with hatred in
  the eye;
  They tried him and condemned him, then led
  him out to die.
  Chorus

4 'Father, now forgive them' — those were the
  words he said;
  In three more days he was alive and risen from
  the dead.
  Chorus

5 He still comes to people, his life moves through
  the lands;
  He uses us for speaking, he touches with
  our hands.
  Chorus

Geoffrey Marshall-Taylor

25

1 When Jesus walked in Galilee,
He gave all men a chance to see
What God intended them to be,
And how they ought to live.

2 When Jesus hung upon the cross,
Enduring hunger, pain and loss,
He looked, with loving eyes, across
The scene, and said, 'Forgive.'

3 When Jesus rose on Easter Day,
He met a woman in the way
And said, 'Go to my friends, and say
The Master is alive.'

4 When Jesus comes to us each day,
And listens to us as we pray,
We'll listen too, and hear him say,
'Come, follow me, and live!'
John Glandfield

26

1 There is singing in the desert,
there is laughter in the skies,
There are wise men filled with wonder,
there are shepherds with surprise,
You can tell the world is dancing
by the light that's in their eyes,
For Jesus Christ is here.

Chorus:
Come and sing aloud your praises,
Come and sing aloud your praises,
Come and sing aloud your praises,
For Jesus Christ is here.

2 He hears deaf men by the lakeside,
   he sees blind men in the streets,
He goes up to those who cannot walk,
   he talks to all he meets,
Touching silken robes or tattered clothes,
   it's everyone he greets,
For Jesus Christ is here.
Chorus

3 There is darkness on the hillside,
   there is sorrow in the town,
There's a man upon a wooden cross,
   a man who's gazing down,
You can see the marks of love
   and not the furrows of a frown,
For Jesus Christ is here.
Chorus

4 There is singing in the desert,
   there is laughter in the skies,
There are wise men filled with wonder,
   there are shepherds with surprise,
You can tell the world is dancing
   by the light that's in their eyes,
For Jesus Christ is here.
Chorus

                    Geoffrey Marshall-Taylor

27 1 There's a child in the streets
         Gives joy to all he meets,
         Full of life, with many friends,
         Works and plays till daylight ends.

         Chorus:
         There's a man for all the people,
         A man whose love is true.
         May this man for all the people
         Help me love others too.

2 There's a preacher in a crowd
Shouts to fishermen out loud,
'Leave your boats and leave the sea,
Come along and work with me.'
Chorus

3 There's a teacher tells a tale,
Makes men argue without fail,
Some are angry, some agree,
When he says, 'You follow me.'
Chorus

4 There's a leader at a feast,
But he says that he's the least,
Rolls his sleeves to wash their feet,
Breaks the bread and tells them, 'Eat.'
Chorus

5 There's a prisoner on a cross
And his friends weep for their loss,
But a soldier with a sword
Says, 'This man has come from God.'
Chorus

6 There's a voice inside a room,
'I have risen from the tomb,
I am bringing you God's peace
And your joy will never cease.'
Chorus

Geoffrey Curtis

28

1 Said Judas to Mary,
'Now what will you do
With your ointment
So rich and so rare?'
'I'll pour it all over
The feet of the Lord,
And I'll wipe it away with my hair,'
She said,
'I'll wipe it away with my hair.'

2 'Oh Mary, oh Mary,
Oh think of the poor —
This ointment, it
Could have been sold.
And think of the blankets
And think of the bread
You could buy with the silver and gold,'
He said,
'You could buy with the silver and gold.'

3 'Tomorrow, tomorrow,
I'll think of the poor,
Tomorrow,' she said,
'Not today.
For dearer than all
Of the poor in the world
Is my love who is going away,'
She said,
'My love who is going away.'

4 Said Jesus to Mary,
'Your love is so deep
Today you may do
As you will.
Tomorrow you say
I am going away,
But my body I leave with you still,'
He said,
'My body I leave with you still.'

5 'The poor of the world
Are my body,' he said,
'To the end of the world
They shall be.
The bread and the blankets
You give to the poor
You'll find you have given to me,'
He said,
'You'll find you have given to me.'

6 'My body will hang
On the cross of the world
Tomorrow,' he said,
'And today,

And Martha and Mary
Will find me again
And wash all my sorrow away,'
He said,
'And wash all my sorrow away.'

Sydney Carter

29

Chorus:
From the darkness came light,
From the blackest of nights;
Wait for the morning, the sunlight, the dawning;
From the darkness came light.

1 Earth so dark and so cold, what great secrets
you hold;
The promise of spring, the wonder you bring
The beauty of nature unfolds.
Chorus

2 Jesus was born in a stall, born to bring light
to us all.
He came to love us, a new life to give us;
Jesus was born in a stall.
Chorus

3 Jesus died on Calvary, suffered for you and me;
He rose from the dark and gloom,
out of a stony tomb,
Walked in the world and was free.
Chorus

4 We have this new life to share, a love to pass
on everywhere;
Time spent in giving, a joy in our living,
In showing to others we care.
Chorus

Jancis Harvey

30

Chorus:
Join with us to sing God's praises,
For His love and for His care,
For the happiness He gives us,
Praise Him for the world we share.

1 Thank Him for the town and country,
Thank Him for the sun and rain,
Thank Him for our homes and gardens,
Sing His praises once again.
Chorus

2 We have eyes to look around us,
We have strength to work and play,
We have voices we can use — to
Sing His praises every day.
Chorus

3 Praise Him in your words of kindness,
Praise Him helping those in need,
Praise Him in your thought for others,
Sing His praises with each deed.
Chorus

Edna Bird

31

1 Can you be sure that the rain will fall?
Can you be sure that birds will fly?
Can you be sure that rivers will flow?
Or that the sun will light the sky?

Chorus:
God has promised.
God never breaks a promise He makes.
His word is always true.

2 Can you be sure that the tide will turn?
Can you be sure that grass will grow?
Can you be sure that night will come,
Or that the sun will melt the snow?
Chorus

3 You can be sure that God is near;
   You can be sure He won't let you down;
   You can be sure He'll always hear;
   And that He's given Jesus, His Son.
   Chorus

                    Geoffrey Marshall-Taylor

32

1 Thank you, Lord, for this new day,
  Thank you, Lord, for this new day,
  Thank you, Lord, for this new day,
  Right where we are.

  Chorus:
  Alleluia, praise the Lord,
  Alleluia, praise the Lord,
  Alleluia, praise the Lord,
  Right where we are.

2 Thank you, Lord, for food to eat,
  Thank you, Lord, for food to eat,
  Thank you, Lord, for food to eat,
  Right where we are.
  Chorus

3 Thank you, Lord, for clothes to wear,
  Thank you, Lord, for clothes to wear,
  Thank you, Lord, for clothes to wear,
  Right where we are.
  Chorus

4 Thank you, Lord, for all your gifts,
  Thank you, Lord, for all your gifts,
  Thank you, Lord, for all your gifts,
  Right where we are.
  Chorus

  Diane Andrew
  adapted by Geoffrey Marshall-Taylor

33

1 Praise the Lord in the rhythm of your music,
Praise the Lord in the freedom of your dance,
Praise the Lord in the country and the city,
Praise Him in the living of your life!

2 Praise the Lord on the organ and piano,
Praise the Lord on guitar and on the drums,
Praise the Lord on the tambourine and cymbals,
Praise Him in the singing of your song!

3 Praise the Lord with the movement of your
bodies,
Praise the Lord with the clapping of your hands,
Praise the Lord with your poetry and painting,
Praise Him in the acting of your play!

4 Praise the Lord in the feeding of the hungry,
Praise the Lord in the healing of disease,
Praise the Lord as you show His love in action,
Praise Him in your caring for the poor!

5 Praise the Lord, every nation, every people,
Praise the Lord, men and women, old and
young,
Praise the Lord, let us celebrate together,
Praise Him everything in heaven and earth!

Peter Casey

34

1 Praise to the Lord, the Almighty,
the King of creation;
O my soul, praise Him, for He is thy
health and salvation;
All ye who hear,
Brothers and sisters draw near,
Praise Him in glad adoration.

2 Praise to the Lord, who o'er all things
so wondrously reigneth;
Shelters thee under His wings, yea,
so gently sustaineth;
Hast thou not seen?
All that is needful hath been
Granted in what He ordaineth.

3 Praise to the Lord, who doth prosper thy work
and defend thee;
Surely his goodness and mercy
will daily attend thee;
Ponder anew
What the Almighty can do,
He who with love doth befriend thee.

4 Praise to the Lord! O let all that is in me
adore Him.
All that hath life and breath, come now
with praises before Him!
Let the Amen
Sound from His people again:
Gladly for aye we adore Him.
Joachim Neander, trans. Catherine Winkworth

35

1 Praise the Lord! you heavens, adore Him;
Praise Him, angels, in the height;
Sun and moon, rejoice before Him,
Praise Him, all you stars and light:
Praise the Lord! for He has spoken,
Worlds His mighty voice obeyed;
Laws, which never shall be broken,
For their guidance He has made.

2 Praise the Lord! for He is glorious;
Never shall His promise fail;
God has made His saints victorious,
Sin and death shall not prevail.
Praise the God of our salvation;
Hosts on high, His power proclaim;
Heaven and earth, and all creation,
Laud and magnify His name!
Foundling Hospital Collection

36

1 God is love; His the care,
Tending each, everywhere.
God is love — all is there!
Jesus came to show Him,
That mankind might know Him:

Chorus:
Sing aloud, loud, loud!
Sing aloud, loud, loud!
God is good! God is truth!
God is beauty! Praise Him!

2 None can see God above;
All have here man to love;
Thus may we Godward move,
Finding him in others,
Holding all men brothers:
Chorus

3 Jesus lived here for men,
Strove and died, rose again,
Rules our hearts, now as then;
For he came to save us
By the truth he gave us:
Chorus

4 To our Lord praise we sing —
Light and life, friend and king,
Coming down love to bring,
Pattern for our duty,
Showing God in beauty:
Chorus

Percy Dearmer

37

1 O praise ye the Lord!
Praise Him in the height;
Rejoice in His word,
Ye angels of light;
Ye heavens, adore Him,
By whom ye were made,
And worship before Him,
In brightness arrayed.

2 O praise ye the Lord!
All things that give sound;
Each jubilant chord,
Re-echo around;
Loud organs, His glory
Forth tell in deep tone,
And sweet harp, the story,
Of what He hath done.

3 O praise ye the Lord!
Thanksgiving and song
To Him be outpoured
All ages along;
For love in creation,
For heaven restored,
For grace of salvation,
O praise ye the Lord!
Sir Henry Baker

38

1 Now thank we all our God,
With heart and hands and voices,
Who wondrous things has done,
In whom His world rejoices;
Who, from our mothers' arms,
Has blessed us on our way
With countless gifts of love,
And still is ours today.

2 O may this bounteous God
Through all our life be near us,
With ever-joyful hearts
And blessed peace to cheer us,
And keep us in His grace,
And guide us when perplexed,
And free us from all ills
In this world and the next.

3 All praise and thanks to God
The Father now be given,
The Son, and Him who reigns
With Them in highest heaven;
The one, eternal God,
Whom earth and heaven adore;
For thus it was, is now,
And shall be ever more.

Martin Rinkart, trans. Catherine Winkworth

39

1 O Lord, all the world belongs to you,
And you are always making all things new.
What is wrong you forgive,
And the new life you give
Is what's turning the world upside down.

2 The world's only loving to its friends,
But your way of loving never ends,
Loving enemies too;
And this loving with you,
Is what's turning the world upside down.

3 The world lives divided and apart,
You draw men together, and we start
In our friendship to see
That in harmony we
Can be turning the world upside down.

4 The world wants the wealth to live in state,
But you show a new way to be great:
Like a servant you came,
And if we do the same,
We'll be turning the world upside down.

5 O Lord, all the world belongs to you,
And you are always making all things new.
What is wrong you forgive,
And the new life you give
Is what's turning the world upside down.

Patrick Appleford

40

1 Praise Him, praise Him,
Praise Him in the morning,
Praise Him in the noon-time,
Praise Him, praise Him,
Praise Him when the sun goes down.

2 Trust Him, trust Him,
Trust Him in the morning,
Trust Him in the noon-time,
Trust Him, trust Him,
Trust Him when the sun goes down.

3 Serve Him, serve Him,
Serve Him in the morning,
Serve Him in the noon-time,
Serve Him, serve Him,
Serve Him when the sun goes down.

4 Praise Him, praise Him,
Praise Him in the morning,
Praise Him in the noon-time,
Praise Him, praise Him,
Praise Him when the sun goes down.

Traditional

41

1 Fill thou my life, O Lord my God,
In every part with praise,
That my whole being may proclaim
Thy being and thy ways.

2 Not for the lip of praise alone,
Nor e'en the praising heart,
I ask, but for a life made up
Of praise in every part:

3 Praise in the common things of life,
Its goings out and in;
Praise in each duty and each deed,
However small and mean.

4 Fill every part of me with praise;
  Let all my being speak
  Of thee and of thy love, O Lord,
  Poor though I be and weak.

5 So shall no part of day or night
  From sacredness be free;
  But all my life, in every step,
  Be fellowship with thee.
                              Horatius Bonar

42

1 Travel on, travel on, there's a river that is
  flowing,
  A river that is flowing night and day.
  Travel on, travel on to the river that is flowing,
  The river will be with you all the way.
  Travel on, travel on to the river that is flowing,
  The river will be with you all the way.

2 Travel on, travel on, there's a flower that is
  growing,
  A flower that is growing night and day.
  Travel on, travel on to the flower that is
  growing,
  The flower will be with you all the way.
  Travel on, travel on to the flower that is
  growing,
  The flower will be with you all the way.

3 Travel on, travel on to the music that is playing,
  The music that is playing night and day.
  Travel on, travel on to the music that is playing,
  The music will be with you all the way.
  Travel on, travel on to the music that is playing,
  The music will be with you all the way.

4 In the kingdom of heaven is my end and my
  beginning
  And the road that I must follow night and day.
  Travel on, travel on to the kingdom that is
  coming,
  The kingdom will be with you all the way.
  Travel on, travel on to the kingdom that is
  coming,
  The kingdom will be with you all the way.

Sydney Carter

43

1 Give me oil in my lamp, keep me burning.
  Give me oil in my lamp, I pray.
  Give me oil in my lamp, keep me burning,
  Keep me burning till the break of day.

  Chorus:
  Sing hosanna, sing hosanna,
  Sing hosanna to the King of Kings!
  Sing hosanna, sing hosanna,
  Sing hosanna to the King!

2 Give me joy in my heart, keep me singing.
  Give me joy in my heart, I pray.
  Give me joy in my heart, keep me singing,
  Keep me singing till the break of day.
  Chorus

3 Give me love in my heart, keep me serving.
  Give me love in my heart, I pray.
  Give me love in my heart, keep me serving,
  Keep me serving till the break of day.
  Chorus

4 Give me peace in my heart, keep me resting.
  Give me peace in my heart, I pray.
  Give me peace in my heart, keep me resting,
  Keep me resting till the break of day.
  Chorus

Traditional

44

1 He who would valiant be
'Gainst all disaster,
Let him in constancy
Follow the Master.
There's no discouragement
Shall make him once relent
His first avowed intent
To be a pilgrim.

2 Who so beset him round
With dismal stories,
Do but themselves confound —
His strength the more is.
No foes shall stay his might,
Though he with giants fight:
He will make good his right
To be a pilgrim.

3 Since, Lord, thou dost defend
Us with thy Spirit,
We know we at the end
Shall life inherit.
Then fancies flee away!
I'll fear not what men say,
I'll labour night and day
To be a pilgrim.

Percy Dearmer, adapted from John Bunyan

45

1 The journey of life
May be easy, may be hard,
There'll be danger on the way;
With Christ at my side
I'll do battle, as I ride,
'Gainst the foe that would lead me astray:

Chorus:
Will you ride, ride, ride
With the King of Kings,
Will you follow my leader true;
Will you shout Hosanna
To the lowly Son of God,
Who died for me and you?

2 My burden is light
And a song is in my heart
As I travel on life's way;
For Christ is my Lord
And he's given me his word
That by my side he'll stay:
Chorus

Valerie Collison

46

1 My faith, it is an oaken staff,
The traveller's well-loved aid;
My faith, it is a weapon stout,
The soldier's trusty blade.
I'll travel on, and still be stirred
To action at my Master's word;
By all my perils undeterred,
A soldier unafraid.

2 My faith, it is an oaken staff,
O let me on it lean;
My faith, it is a trusty sword,
May falsehood find it keen.
Thy spirit, Lord, to me impart,
O make me what thou ever art,
Of patient and courageous heart,
As all true saints have been.

Thomas Lynch

47

1 One more step along the world I go,
One more step along the world I go,
From the old things to the new
Keep me travelling along with you.

Chorus:
And it's from the old I travel to the new,
Keep me travelling along with you.

2 Round the corners of the world I turn,
More and more about the world I learn.
And the new things that I see
You'll be looking at along with me.
Chorus

3 As I travel through the bad and good
Keep me travelling the way I should.
Where I see no way to go
You'll be telling me the way, I know.
Chorus

4 Give me courage when the world is rough,
Keep me loving though the world is tough.
Leap and sing in all I do,
Keep me travelling along with you.
Chorus

5 You are older than the world can be
You are younger than the life in me.
Ever old and ever new,
Keep me travelling along with you.
Chorus

Sydney Carter

48

1 Father, hear the prayer we offer:
  Not for ease that prayer shall be,
  But for strength that we may ever
  Live our lives courageously.

2 Not for ever in green pastures
  Do we ask our way to be;
  But the steep and rugged pathway
  May we tread rejoicingly.

3 Not for ever by still waters
  Would we idly rest and stay;
  But would smite the living fountains
  From the rocks along our way.

4 Be our strength in hours of weakness,
  In our wanderings be our guide;
  Through endeavour, failure, danger,
  Father, be thou at our side.
                              Love Willis

49

1 We are climbing Jesus' ladder, ladder,
  We are climbing Jesus' ladder, ladder,
  We are climbing Jesus' ladder, ladder,
  Children of the Lord.

  Chorus:
  So let's all
  Rise and shine and give God the glory, glory,
  Rise and shine and give God the glory, glory,
  Rise and shine and give God the glory, glory,
  Children of the Lord.

2 We are following where he leads us, leads us,
  We are following where he leads us, leads us,
  We are following where he leads us, leads us,
  Children of the Lord.
  Chorus

3 We are reaching out to others, others,
We are reaching out to others, others,
We are reaching out to others, others,
Children of the Lord.
Chorus

4 We are one with all who serve Him, serve Him,
We are one with all who serve Him, serve Him,
We are one with all who serve Him, serve Him,
Children of the Lord.
Chorus

Traditional (adapted)

50

1 When a knight won his spurs in the stories of
old,
He was gentle and brave, he was gallant and
bold;
With a shield on his arm and a lance in his hand,
For God and for valour he rode through the
land.

2 No charger have I, and no sword by my side,
Yet still to adventure and battle I ride,
Though back into storyland giants have fled,
And the knights are no more and the dragons
are dead.

3 Let faith be my shield and let joy be my steed
'Gainst the dragons of anger, the ogres of greed;
And let me set free, with the sword of my youth,
From the castle of darkness, the power of
the truth.

Jan Struther

51 Our Father, who art in heaven,
  Hallowed be thy name;
Thy kingdom come, thy will be done,
  Hallowed be thy name,
On the earth as it is in heaven,
  Hallowed be thy name.
Give us this day our daily bread,
  Hallowed be thy name.
Forgive us all our trespasses,
  Hallowed be thy name,
As we forgive those who trespass against us,
  Hallowed be thy name;
And lead us not into temptation,
  Hallowed be thy name,
But deliver us from all that is evil,
  Hallowed be thy name;
For thine is the kingdom, the power and the glory,
  Hallowed be thy name,
For ever and for ever and ever,
  Hallowed be thy name.
Amen, Amen, it shall be so,
  Hallowed be thy name;
Amen, Amen, it shall be so,
  Hallowed be thy name.

Traditional Caribbean

52 1 Lord of all hopefulness, Lord of all joy,
  Whose trust ever child-like, no cares
  could destroy,
  Be there at our waking, and give us, we pray,
  Your bliss in our hearts, Lord, at the break
  of the day.

2 Lord of all eagerness, Lord of all faith,
  Whose strong hands were skilled at the plane
  and the lathe,
  Be there at our labours, and give us, we pray,
  Your strength in our hearts, Lord, at the noon
  of the day.

3 Lord of all kindliness, Lord of all grace,
Your hands swift to welcome, your arms to
embrace,
Be there at our homing, and give us, we pray,
Your love in our hearts, Lord, at the eve
of the day.

4 Lord of all gentleness, Lord of all calm,
Whose voice is contentment, whose presence
is balm,
Be there at our sleeping, and give us, we pray,
Your peace in our hearts, Lord, at the end
of the day.

Jan Struther

53

1 Peace, perfect peace, is the gift of Christ
our Lord.
Peace, perfect peace, is the gift of Christ
our Lord.
Thus, says the Lord, will the world know
my friends,
Peace, perfect peace, is the gift of Christ
our Lord.

2 Hope, perfect hope, is the gift of Christ our Lord.
Hope, perfect hope, is the gift of Christ our Lord.
Thus, says the Lord, will the world know
my friends,
Hope, perfect hope, is the gift of Christ our Lord.

3 Joy, perfect joy, is the gift of Christ our Lord.
Joy, perfect joy, is the gift of Christ our Lord.
Thus, says the Lord, will the world know
my friends,
Joy, perfect joy, is the gift of Christ our Lord.

Kevin Mayhew

54

1 The King of love my shepherd is,
  Whose goodness faileth never;
  I nothing lack if I am His
  And He is mine for ever.

2 Where streams of living water flow
  My ransomed soul He leadeth,
  And where the verdant pastures grow
  With food celestial feedeth.

3 Perverse and foolish oft I strayed;
  But yet in love He sought me,
  And on His shoulder gently laid,
  And home rejoicing brought me.

4 In death's dark vale I fear no ill,
  With thee, dear Lord, beside me;
  Thy rod and staff my comfort still,
  Thy cross before to guide me.

5 And so through all the length of days
  Thy goodness faileth never;
  Good shepherd, may I sing thy praise
  Within thy house for ever!
  Sir Henry Baker

55

1 Colours of day dawn into the mind,
  The sun has come up, the night is behind.
  Go down in the city, into the street,
  And let's give the message to the people we meet.

  Chorus:
  So light up the fire and let the flame burn,
  Open the door, let Jesus return.
  Take seeds of his Spirit, let the fruit grow,
  Tell the people of Jesus, let his love show.

2 Go through the park, on into the town;
  The sun still shines on, it never goes down.
  The light of the world is risen again;
  The people of darkness are needing our friend.
  Chorus

3 Open your eyes, look into the sky,
The darkness has come, the sun came to die.
The evening draws on, the sun disappears,
But Jesus is living, his Spirit is near.
Chorus

Susan McClellan, John Pac and Keith Ryecroft

56

1 The Lord's my shepherd, I'll not want;
He makes me down to lie
In pastures green; He leadeth me
The quiet waters by.

2 My soul He doth restore again,
And me to walk doth make
Within the paths of righteousness,
E'en for His own name's sake.

3 Yea, though I walk in death's dark vale,
Yet will I fear no ill;
For thou art with me, and thy rod
And staff me comfort still.

4 Goodness and mercy all my life
Shall surely follow me,
And in God's house for evermore
My dwelling-place shall be.

Scottish Psalter

57

1 Think of all the things we lose,
So many things, I get confused:
Our pencil sharpeners, favourite books,
Our indoor shoes and outdoor boots,
Pocket money down the drain,
Then felt-tip pens and people's names.
The worst of all things to be lost
Is just a friend you really trust.

2 Think of all the things we find,
So many things I bring to mind:
In lofts and cupboards, if you browse,
Are old tin whistles, acting clothes,
Clocks that used to chime, and bits
Of engines and of building kits:
But even better, I believe,
Is just a friend to share them with.

3 Think of times we lose our nerves,
We're feeling sad and no-one cares:
An empty feeling deep inside,
There's nowhere else for us to hide.
That's the time to call a friend
Whom we can never lose again:
There's one friend who is very near,
A friend who takes away our fear.

Tom McGuinness (adapted)

58

1 At the name of Jesus
Every knee shall bow,
Every tongue confess him
King of glory now;
'Tis the Father's pleasure
We should call him Lord,
Who from the beginning
Was the mighty Word.

2 Humbled for a season,
To receive a name
From the lips of sinners
Unto whom he came,
Faithfully he bore it
Spotless to the last,
Brought it back victorious
When from death he passed.

3 Name him, brothers, name him,
With love as strong as death,
But with awe and wonder,
And with bated breath;
He is God and Saviour,
He is Christ the Lord,
Ever to be worshipped,
Trusted and adored.

4 In your hearts enthrone him;
There let him subdue
All that is not holy,
All that is not true:
Crown him as your captain
In temptation's hour;
Let his will enfold you
In its light and power.

Caroline Noel

59

Chorus:
I will bring to you the best gift I can offer;
I will sing to you the best things in my mind.

1 Paper pictures, bits of string, I'll bring you
almost anything,
I'll bring a song that only I can sing:
The rainbow colours in the sky, the misty moon
that caught my eye,
The magic of a new-born butterfly.
Chorus

2 I'll bring a song of winter trees, the skidding ice,
the frozen leaves,
The battles in our snowball-shouting streets.
I'll bring you summers I have known, adventure
trips and journeys home,
The summer evenings playing down our road.
Chorus

3 I'll share my secrets and my dreams, I'll show
  you wonders I have seen,
  And I will listen when you speak your name;
  And if you really want me to, I will share my
  friends with you,
  Everyone at home and in my school.
  Chorus

  Tom McGuinness

60

1 In the morning early
  I go down to the sea
  And see the mist on the shore;
  I listen, and I listen.

2 When I go to the rocks
  I go looking for shells
  And feel the sand beneath my feet;
  I listen, and I listen.

3 When the stormy day comes
  Waves crash on the cliffs
  And the wind whistles through my hair;
  I listen, and I listen.

4 And at night when I sleep
  And the sea is calm
  The gentle waves lap the shore;
  I listen, and I listen.

5 I sometimes think that God
  Is talking to me
  When I hear the sound of the sea;
  I listen, and I listen.
  I listen, and I listen.

  Hazel Charlton

61

1 All over the world,
Everywhere,
Where the sun shines,
And where the white snow gleams;
In the green, green forests and by the streams,
Hands are busy, plans are laid,
And slowly, slowly,
Somewhere, somebody's house is made.

Chorus:
Everybody's building, everybody's building,
Everybody's building, day by day,
Everybody's building, everybody's building,
Everybody's building in a different way.

2 All over the world,
Everywhere,
Where the sun shines,
And where the darkest night
Holds back the coming of the morning light:
Bricks are laid and wood is sawn,
And slowly, slowly,
Out of a dream a house is born.
Chorus

3 All over the world,
Everywhere,
Where we're living,
Wherever children grow,
And their lives are shaped as the moments go,
Minds are building, plans are laid,
And slowly, slowly,
Somewhere somebody's life is made.
Chorus

4 All over the world,
Everywhere,
Where we're living,
Wherever children play,
For the things they do and the things they say,
For good or ill, ground is laid,
And slowly, slowly,
Somewhere, somebody's life is made.
Chorus   *David Winter*

62

1 Heavenly Father, may thy blessing
Rest upon thy children now,
When in praise thy name they hallow,
When in prayer to thee they bow;
In the wondrous story reading
Of the Lord of truth and grace,
May they see thy love reflected
In the light of his dear face.

2 May they learn from this great story
All the arts of friendliness;
Truthful speech and honest action,
Courage, patience, steadfastness;
How to master self and temper,
How to make their conduct fair;
When to speak and when be silent,
When to do and when forbear.

3 May his spirit wise and holy
With his gifts their spirits bless,
Make them loving, joyous, peaceful,
Rich in goodness, gentleness,
Strong in self-control, and faithful,
Kind in thought and deed; for he
Sayeth, 'What ye do for others
Ye are doing unto me.'
                    William Charter-Piggott

63

Chorus:
Spirit of God, as strong as the wind,
Gentle as is the dove,
Give us your joy, and give us your peace,
Show to us Jesus' love.

1 You inspired men, long, long ago,
They then proclaimed your word;
We see their lives, serving mankind:
Through them your voice is heard.
Chorus

2 Without your help, we fail our Lord,
We cannot live His way,
We need your power, we need your strength,
Following Christ each day.
Chorus

Margaret Old
adapted by Geoffrey Marshall-Taylor

64

1 The wise may bring their learning,
The rich may bring their wealth,
And some may bring their greatness,
And some their strength and health:
We too would bring our treasures
To offer to the King;
We have no wealth or learning,
What gifts then shall we bring?

2 We'll bring the many duties
We have to do each day;
We'll try our best to please Him,
At home, at school, at play:
And better are these treasures
To offer to the King,
Than richest gifts without them;
Yet these we all may bring.

3 We'll bring Him hearts that love Him,
We'll bring Him thankful praise,
And lives for ever striving
To follow in His ways:
And these shall be the treasures
We offer to the King,
And these are gifts that ever
Our grateful hearts may bring.

Book of Praise for Children (adapted)

65

1 When I needed a neighbour, were you there,
were you there?
When I needed a neighbour, were you there?

Chorus:
And the creed and the colour and the name
won't matter,
Were you there?

2 I was hungry and thirsty, were you there,
were you there?
I was hungry and thirsty, were you there?
Chorus

3 I was cold, I was naked, were you there,
were you there?
I was cold, I was naked, were you there?
Chorus

4 When I needed a shelter, were you there,
were you there?
When I needed a shelter, were you there?
Chorus

5 When I needed a healer, were you there,
were you there?
When I needed a healer, were you there?
Chorus

6 Wherever you travel, I'll be there, I'll be there,
Wherever you travel, I'll be there.

Chorus:
And the creed and the colour and the name
won't matter,
I'll be there.

Sydney Carter

66

1 In Christ there is no east or west,
In him no south or north,
But one great fellowship of love
Throughout the whole wide earth.

2 In him shall true hearts everywhere
Their high communion find;
His service is the golden cord
Close-binding all mankind.

3 Join hands, then, brothers of the faith,
Whate'er your race may be!
Who serves my Father as a son
Is surely kin to me.

4 In Christ now meet both east and west,
In him meet south and north;
All Christly souls are one in him,
Throughout the whole wide earth.

John Oxenham

67

1 The ink is black, the page is white,
Together we learn to read and write,
   to read and write;
And now a child can understand
This is the law of all the land,
   all the land;
The ink is black, the page is white,
Together we learn to read and write,
   to read and write.

2 The slate is black, the chalk is white,
The words stand out so clear and bright,
   so clear and bright;
And now at last we plainly see
The alphabet of liberty,
   liberty;
The slate is black, the chalk is white,
Together we learn to read and write,
   to read and write.

3 A child is black, a child is white,
   The whole world looks upon the sight,
      upon the sight;
   For very well the whole world knows,
   This is the way that freedom grows,
      freedom grows;
   A child is black, a child is white,
   Together we learn to read and write,
      to read and write.

4 The world is black, the world is white,
   It turns by day and then by night,
      and then by night;
   It turns so each and every one
   Can take his station in the sun,
      in the sun;
   The world is black, the world is white,
   Together we learn to read and write,
      to read and write.

David Arkin

68

1 Kum ba yah, my Lord, Kum ba yah,
   Kum ba yah, my Lord, Kum ba yah,
   Kum ba yah, my Lord, Kum ba yah,
   O Lord, Kum ba yah.

2 Someone's crying, Lord, Kum ba yah,
   Someone's crying, Lord, Kum ba yah,
   Someone's crying, Lord, Kum ba yah,
   O Lord, Kum ba yah.

3 Someone's singing, Lord, Kum ba yah,
   Someone's singing, Lord, Kum ba yah,
   Someone's singing, Lord, Kum ba yah,
   O Lord, Kum ba yah.

4 Someone's praying, Lord, Kum ba yah,
   Someone's praying, Lord, Kum ba yah,
   Someone's praying, Lord, Kum ba yah,
   O Lord, Kum ba yah.

Traditional

69

1 I belong to a family, the biggest on earth,
Ten thousand every day are coming to birth.
Our name isn't Davis or Groves or Jones,
It's the name every man should be proud he owns:

Chorus:
It's the family of man, keeps growing,
The family of man, keeps sowing
The seeds of a new life every day.

2 I've got a sister in Melbourne, and brother
in Delhi,
The whole wide world is dad and mother to me.
Wherever you turn you will find my kin,
Whatever the creed or the colour of skin:
Chorus

3 The miner in the Rhondda, the coolie in Peking,
Men across the world who reap and plough
and spin,
They've got a life and others to share it,
Let's bridge the oceans and declare it:
Chorus

4 Some people say the world is a horrible place,
But it's just as good or bad as the human race;
Dirt and misery or health and joy,
Man can build or can destroy:
Chorus

Karl Dallas

70

1 Would you walk by on the other side,
When someone called for aid?
Would you walk by on the other side,
And would you be afraid?

Chorus:
Cross over the road, my friend,
Ask the Lord His strength to lend,
His compassion has no end,
Cross over the road.

2 Would you walk by on the other side,
When you saw a loved one stray?
Would you walk by on the other side,
Or would you watch and pray?
Chorus

3 Would you walk by on the other side,
When starving children cried?
Would you walk by on the other side
And would you not provide?
Chorus

Pamela Verrall

71

1 If I had a hammer, I'd hammer in the morning,
I'd hammer in the evening, all over this land;
I'd hammer out danger, I'd hammer out a
warning,
I'd hammer out love between my brothers
and my sisters,
All over this land.

2 If I had a bell, I'd ring it in the morning,
I'd ring it in the evening, all over this land;
I'd ring out danger, I'd ring out a warning,
I'd ring out love between my brothers and my sisters,
All over this land.

3 If I had a song, I'd sing it in the morning,
  I'd sing it in the evening, all over this land;
  I'd sing out danger, I'd sing out a warning,
  I'd sing out love between my brothers and my sisters,
  All over this land.

4 Well I've got a hammer, and I've got a bell,
  And I'm going to sing all over this land;
  It's the hammer of justice, it's the bell of freedom,
  It's the song about love between my brothers and my sisters,
  All over this land.

Words: Lee Hays Music: Pete Seeger

72

1 Every word comes alive,
  When it's written or read;
  There is life in a word,
  When it's sung or said.
  But there can't be a living word
  Never seen or never heard,
  But only when
  It gives itself
  To tongue and . . . pen!
      And a tune is alive
      When it's played or sung;
      It will even thrive
      Whistled, scraped or rung.
      Then it meets the word, and wakes;
      As you strike the notes, it breaks
      Into a living song.

2 But a song must grow
  In a singer too,
  And it needs to flow
  Into me and you.
  For it's lost and it can't be found
  If we never make it sound,
  So take a chance
  And lift the song to
  Make it . . . dance!

Now the word's in me,
And I make it shout,
And the tune rings free
As I peal it out.
And the words and the tune are one,
Singing me as I sing it on,
For I'm a living song.

Arthur Scholey

73

1 When your Father made the world, before that world was old,
In his eye what he had made was lovely to behold.
Help your people to care for your world.

Chorus:
The world is a garden you made,
And you are the one who planted the seed,
The world is a garden you made,
A life for our food, life for our joy,
Life we could kill with our selfish greed.

2 And the world that he had made, the seas, the rocks, the air,
All the creatures and the plants he gave into our care.
Help your people to care for your world.
Chorus

3 When you walked in Galilee, you said your Father knows
When each tiny sparrow dies, each fragile lily grows.
Help your people to care for your world.
Chorus

4 And the children of the earth, like sheep within your fold,
Should have food enough to eat, and shelter from the cold.
Help your people to care for your world.
Chorus

Ann Conlon

This was written for the World Wide Fund for Nature.

74

1 Sad, puzzled eyes of small, hungry children,
  Thin, weary bodies tending the ground;
  Weak, pleading voices begging in cities;
  They long for the day when food is shared
  round.

  Chorus:
  Prayers of sorrow, prayers of loving,
  Looking for ways to give and to share.
  Learning, explaining, helping, supporting;
  Show all the world how deeply we care.

2 Rumbling earthquakes, villages topple;
  Drought shrivels cattle, harvests and men,
  Flood waters swirling, drowning and surging,
  Despairing survivors begin life again.
  Chorus

3 Terror and death in war shattered countries,
  Misery, tears, deep longing for peace.
  Refugees flee — no hope for the future;
  How long must they wait for suffering to
  cease?
  Chorus

Ann Sutcliffe

75

1 I saw the man from Galilee
  Who told a message new.
  The hungry crowd had gathered round,
  To see what he could do.
  And in his words was hope;
  And in his hands was bread.
  'Come, share this bread,
  And share my life —
  My life for you,' he said.

2 I saw a boy with barley loaves;
  He had some small fish too.
  'I can't do much, but I can share:
  Lord Jesus, it's for you.
  For in your words is hope
  And in your hands is bread.
  I'll share my bread,
  And know your love —
  Your life for me,' he said.

3 I saw a rich young man, who came
  To speak to Jesus too.
  'I want to live, I don't know how,'
  He said, 'What can I do?'
  And Jesus answered, 'This
  Is life, to share your bread.
  Sell all you have,
  Give to the poor,
  Life can be yours,' he said.

4 I saw the whole world in the eyes
  Of one small hungry boy.
  There is no hope, there is no life,
  There is no sign of joy.
  And how can there be hope,
  Where people have no bread?
  They struggle on,
  And try to live,
  But life hangs by a thread.
    Yet Jesus shows us hope,
    For in his hands is bread;
    Bread for the world,
    If all will share:
    He is the living bread.

George A. Chalmers

76

1 God in his love for us lent us this planet.
Gave it a purpose in time and in space:
Small as a spark from the fire of creation,
Cradle of life and the home of our race.

2 Thanks be to God for its bounty and beauty,
Life that sustains us in body and mind:
Plenty for all, if we learn how to share it,
Riches undreamed of to fathom and find.

3 Long have the wars of man ruined its harvest:
Long has earth bowed to the terror of force:
Long have we wasted what others have need
of,
Poisoned the fountain of life at its source.

4 Earth is the Lord's: it is ours to enjoy it.
Ours, as his stewards, to farm and defend.
From its pollution, misuse, and destruction.
Good Lord, deliver us, world without end!

Fred Pratt Green

77

1 The sun burns hot and dry
High in the cloudless sky,
No shade.
The soil is crumbling dust,
Like powder at the touch.

2 The brittle corn is crushed,
Away blow empty husks,
No food.
No life left in the grain,
The seed has failed again.

3 Empty hands, reaching out,
But there's nothing there.
Cracking lips,
Withered skin,
The eyes just stare.

4 The cows and goats are thin,
  The bones show through the skin,
  No milk.
  They search for grass to graze,
  They swelter in the haze.

5 The wells are empty holes,
  The river only stones,
  No drink.
  When will a storm cloud burst
  To satisfy the thirst?

6 Then it came, cooling rain,
  Falling all around;
  Everywhere,
  Muddy pools, form in the ground.

7 The desert dances on,
  Now water has come down,
  New life.
  And seeds of hope begin.
  How long will be the spring?
  How long will be the spring?
                    Geoffrey Gardner

78 1 By brother sun who brings the day,
         And sheds his dazzling light,
         And warms the world with welcome ray;
         By sister moon and sister stars,
         Who turn throughout the night,
         Above in heaven as they shine:
         Be praised by all your creatures, Lord,
         To you all praise belongs!

2 By brother wind and brother air
  On cloudy days and bright,
  In weather stormy, calm or fair;
  By sister water, precious pure,
  Whose taste is cool delight —
  Most humble yet reviving drink:
  Be praised by all your creatures, Lord,
  To you all praise belongs!

3 By brother fire, robust and strong,
  Who gives us heat and might,
  With you now join we all our song,
  And with our sister earth as well,
  With whom we all unite
  To sing with flowers, fruit and grass:
  Be praised by all your creatures, Lord,
  To you all praise belongs!

David Self

This is based on a poem by St Francis of Assisi.

79

1 (1) From the tiny ant,
  (2) *From the tiny ant,*
  (1) To the elephant,
  (2) *To the elephant,*
  (1) From the snake to the kangaroo,
  (2) *From the snake to the kangaroo,*
  (1) From the great white shark,
  (2) *From the great white shark,*
  (1) To the singing lark,
  (2) *To the singing lark,*
  (1) Care for them, it's up to you
  (2) *Care for them, it's up to you,*
  (1 & 2) Care for them it's up to you,
  (1 & 2) Care for them it's up to you.
  (1 & 2) No one else will care for them,
  (1) It's up
  (2) *It's up*
  (1 & 2) It's up to you.

2 (1) From the tabby cat,
(2) *From the tabby cat,*
(1) To the desert rat,
(2) *To the desert rat,*
(1) From the hamster to the chimpanzee,
(2) *From the hamster to the chimpanzee,*
(1) From the common tern,
(2) *From the common tern,*
(1) To the crawling worm,
(2) *To the crawling worm,*
(1) Care for them, it's up to me,
(2) *Care for them, it's up to me,*
(1 & 2) Care for them it's up to me,
(1 & 2) Care for them it's up to me.
(1 & 2) No one else will care for them,
(1) It's up
(2) *It's up*
(1 & 2) It's up to me.

3 (1) From the mongrel dog,
(2) *From the mongrel dog,*
(1) To the snorting hog,
(2) *To the snorting hog,*
(1) From the badger to the platypus,
(2) *From the badger to the platypus,*
(1) From the small minnow,
(2) *From the small minnow,*
(1) To the white rhino,
(2) *To the white rhino,*
(1) Care for them it's up to us,
(2) *Care for them it's up to us,*
(1 & 2) Care for them it's up to us,
(1 & 2) Care for them it's up to us.
(1 & 2) No one else will care for them,
(1) It's up
(2) *It's up*
(1 & 2) It's up to us.

Geoffrey Gardner

*This song can be sung by two groups, indicated by
(1) and (2). Generally, group (2) echoes group
(1). If you prefer, everyone can sing every line.*

80

1 All the animals that I have ever seen,
  Big ones, little ones, and others in between,
  Four legs, two legs,
  Some no legs at all;
  I like them all.

2 All the animals that like your strokes and pats,
  Dogs and hamsters, gerbils, guinea pigs and
  cats,
  Mice and tortoises,
  Rabbits in the hutch;
  I like so much.

3 All the animals that fly up in the sky,
  Robins, wrens, and butterflies that flutter by,
  Magpies, dragonflies,
  And the bumble bee;
  I like to see.

4 All the animals I only see at night,
  Hedgehog, nightingale and owl with eyes so
  bright.
  Fox and badger,
  Moths and bat and shrew;
  I like them too.

5 All the animals that live beneath the sea,
  Shrimps and prawns and jellyfish that tickle
  me,
  Starfish, anemones,
  Crabs beneath my feet!
  I like to meet.

6 There are animals I'll never see at all,
  Some live overseas, and some are just too
  small,
  All God's animals,
  Need the care we give,
  If they're to live.

Simon Fitter

81

1 What about being old Moses
And slogging across the sand,
Escaping through the wilderness
To reach the Promised Land?

To be old Moses would be a mistake;
Today the fun of it is
That we've only one world and we can make
Our Promised Land from this!

2 What about being Saint Brendon,
For mile after nautical mile,
He plunged across fantastic seas
In search of the Blessed Isle?

To be Saint Brendon would be a mistake;
Today the fun of it is
That we've only one world and we can make
Our blessed isle from this!

3 What about being Columbus
And seeking another way round,
With oceans still to voyage on,
And more new worlds to be found?

To be Columbus would be a mistake;
Today the fun of it is
That we've only one world and we can make
Our new world out of this!

4 What about taking a space-ship
And flying to space unknown.
There must be worlds enough to give
Us each one of his own?

To take a space-ship would be a mistake;
Today the fun of it is
That we've only one world and we can make
Our one world out of this!

Arthur Scholey

St Brendon (484–577 A.D.) was an Irish Christian who sailed for several years to find 'paradise amid the waves'. Christopher Columbus (1451–1506) was an Italian explorer.

82

1 It's the springs up in the mountains make the
  rivers of the plain,
  That bring water to the cities as they seek the
  sea again,
  And the rivers fill the oceans and the oceans
  make the rain.
  By the winds blowing over one world.

  Chorus:
  And a man becomes a neighbour or a brother
  or a friend,
  When the one-ness of the world you understand.
  And the east for your neighbour is another
  neighbour's west.
  It depends upon just where you stand.

2 There are people in the mountains and the
  valleys down below,
  There are people in the tropics, there are
  people in the snow,
  Some are happy, some are homeless folk who
  have no place to go,
  But we all have to live in one world.
  Chorus

3 There are workers for their wages out in field
  and factory,
  There are fishers for our food supply in boats
  upon the sea;
  There are people still imprisoned in the cage of
  poverty,
  As we labour for life in one world.
  Chorus

4 As the sun lights up the morning, and another
  day is found,
  It's a gift to all that's living, that the world still
  spins around,
  And the night is still the day but seen the other
  way around,
  As the sun shines upon this one world.
  Chorus

Richard Tysoe

83

Chorus:
I'm going to paint a perfect picture,
A world of make believe;
No more hunger, war or suffering,
The world I'd like to see.

1 The blackbird sings in the hedgerow,
   The white owl sleeps in the barn,
   The brown geese fly, a group in the sky,
   The yellow chick pecks the corn.
   Chorus

2 The stream runs clear through the meadow,
   The wheat ears swell with the grain,
   The oak trees give them shelter and shade,
   The sunlight bursts through the rain.
   Chorus

3 The farmers gather the harvest,
   The children play by the mill,
   The cattle chew and flick up their tails,
   The ponies graze on the hill.

   Chorus
   I'm going to paint a perfect picture,
   A world of make believe;
   No more hunger, war or suffering,
   The world I'd like to see,
   The world I'd like to see.

Geoffrey Gardner

*This song describes a world where all races (verse
1), all the world's resources (verse 2) and all the
world's creatures (verse 3) are in perfect
harmony.*

84

1 Waves are beating on the shore,
  Crashing into foam,
  Seagulls squealing, wheeling high,
  Sailors coming home.
  Boats are bobbing up and down,
  Safe in harbour now,
  Some are riding out the storm,
  Dipping bow on bow.

2 God has made the sea so vast,
  Ocean's roaring swell;
  Cliffs of chalk and granite rocks,
  Sailors know them well;
  Furl the sails and winch the sheets,
  Feel the salt spray fly,
  Know the freedom of the sea,
  Underneath the sky.

3 Ever since the world began,
  People sailed the seas,
  Plunged across the roaring tides,
  Floated on the breeze;
  Feel the decks beneath your feet,
  See the golden sand,
  Set your feet upon the shore,
  Coming home to land.
                    Copyright controlled

85

1 Spirit of peace, come to our waiting world;
  Throughout the nations, may your voice be
  heard.
  Unlock the door of hope, for you hold the key;
  Spirit of peace, come to our world.

2 Spirit of love, come to our waiting world;
  Throughout the nations, may your voice be
  heard.
  Unlock the door of hope, for you hold the key;
  Spirit of love, come to our world.

3 Spirit of strength, come to our waiting world;
   Throughout the nations, may your voice be
   heard.
   Unlock the door of hope, for you hold the key;
   Spirit of strength, come to our world.

4 Spirit of light, come to our waiting world;
   Throughout the nations, may your voice be
   heard.
   Unlock the door of hope, for you hold the key;
   Spirit of light, come to our world.

5 Spirit of God, come to our waiting world;
   Throughout the nations, may your voice be
   heard.
   Unlock the door of hope, for you hold the key;
   Spirit of God, come to our world.
   Spirit of God, come to our world.

Geoffrey Gardner

86 1 The bell of creation is swinging for ever,
   In all of the things that are coming to be,
   The bell of creation is swinging for ever,
   And all of the while it is swinging in me.

   Chorus:
   Swing, bell, over the land!
   Swing, bell, under the sea!
   The bell of creation is swinging for ever,
   And all of the while it is swinging in me.

2 In all of my loving, in all of my labour
   In all of the things that are coming to be,
   In all of my loving, in all of my labour,
   The bell of creation is swinging in me.
   Chorus

3 I look to the life that is living for ever
In all of the things that are coming to be,
I look to the life that is living for ever
And all of the while it is looking for me.
Chorus

4 I'll swing with the bell that is swinging for ever,
In all of the things that are coming to be,
I'll swing with the bell that is swinging for ever,
And all of the while it is swinging in me.
Chorus

Sydney Carter

87

1 Give us hope, Lord, for each day,
Give us hope, Lord, for each day,
Guide our footsteps on the way,
Give us hope, Lord, for each day.

2 Give us strength, Lord, for each day . . .

3 Give us peace, Lord, for each day . . .

4 Give us love, Lord, for each day . . .

5 Give us joy, Lord, for each day . . .

Alternative words

1 Give us friends, Lord, for each day,
Give us friends, Lord, for each day,
Make us thankful on the way,
Give us friends, Lord, for each day.

2 Give us food, Lord, for each day . . .

3 Give us homes, Lord, for each day . . .

4 Give us clothes, Lord, for each day . . .
Geoffrey Gardner

The words by Geoffrey Gardner appear with the agreement of David Lynch, the composer of the music. David Lynch has requested that his original words, known as 'The Bell Song', be printed in addition.

The Bell Song

1 You gotta have love in your heart;
   You gotta have love in your heart;
   You knew it was Jesus right from the start;
   You gotta have love in your heart.

2 You gotta have peace on your mind;
   You gotta have peace on your mind;
   You knew it was Jesus there all the time;
   You gotta have peace on your mind.

3 You gotta have joy in your soul;
   You gotta have joy in your soul;
   The love of Jesus will make you whole;
   You gotta have peace in your soul.
                    David Lynch

88

1 I was lying in the roadway,
   Beaten, robbed and left to die,
   When someone passed the other side —
   I tried to catch his eye;
   But he kept staring straight ahead
   And quickly scurried by.
     Was that you, my friend,
     Was that you?
     Was that you, my friend,
     Was that you?
     Oh, I really was in need —
     Was that you?
     Was that you?

2 I was crying in the roadway,
 Freezing cold and gripped in pain,
 Then someone came across to see —
 I dared to hope again;
 But he just looked and hurried on
 And left me in the rain.
   Was that you, my friend,
   Was that you?
   Was that you, my friend,
   Was that you?
   Oh, I really was in need —
   Was that you?
   Was that you?

3 I was dying in the roadway,
 And at last I knew despair,
 For now, I saw with fading eyes,
 My enemy stood there —
 But then he knelt, and lifted me,
 And brought me safely here.
   That was you, my friend,
   That was you!
   That was you, my friend,
   That was you!
   Oh, you were a friend in deed —
   That was you!
   That was you!

Arthur Scholey

*A song based on the parable of the Good
Samaritan (Luke 10.)*

89

1 Guess how I feel,
Sometimes,
Nothing is real
Sometimes,
Everyone's living in dreams.
Know what I think
Sometimes,
I've lost the link
Sometimes,
Nothing makes sense, so it seems:
We've all become strange machines.
But then I

Chorus
Look in the sky,
Tell all the clouds to pass on by.
The sun will be there
Even if you can't see it,
Always be there,
I can guarantee it.

2 How about you,
Sometimes?
Are you lost, too,
Sometimes?
Caught up in roundabout schemes?
Gives this a try
Sometimes,
Set your sights high
Sometimes,
Simply try changing the scene,
I'm sure you know what I mean.

Chorus
Look in the sky,
Tell all the clouds to pass on by.
The sun will be there
Even if you can't see it,
Always be there,
I can guarantee it,
Every time.

David Stoll

90

1 I come like a beggar with a gift in my hand;
I come like a beggar with a gift in my hand.
By the hungry I will feed you,
By the poor I'll make you rich,
By the broken I will mend you.
Tell me,
Which one is which?

2 I come like a prisoner to bring you the key,
I come like a prisoner to bring you the key.
By the hungry I will feed you,
By the poor I'll make you rich,
By the broken I will mend you.
Tell me,
Which one is which?

3 The need of another is the gift that I bring,
The need of another is the gift that I bring.
By the hungry I will feed you,
By the poor I'll make you rich,
By the broken I will mend you.
Tell me,
Which one is which?

4 Take the wine that I bring you and the bread
that I break,
Take the wine that I bring you and the bread
that I break.
By the hungry I will feed you,
By the poor I'll make you rich,
By the broken I will mend you.
Tell me,
Which one is which?

Sydney Carter

91

1 You can build a wall around you,
Stone by stone, a solid ring;
You can live alone, in an empty home,
Be in charge and be the king.

Chorus:
Break out, reach out,
Make the walls crumble down, down, down.
Break out, reach out,
Make the walls tumble down.

2 You can build a wall around you,
Stop the sun from shining in;
There'll be snow-topped trees and a chilling
breeze,
Always winter, never spring.
Chorus

3 You can build a wall around you,
Slam the door shut fast and firm;
There's no friend at hand who can understand,
To love you, and help you learn.
Chorus

Geoffrey Gardner

*This is based on Oscar Wilde's story 'The selfish
giant'.*

92

1 When night arrives and chills the skies,
And stillness settles across the land,
The hazy moon shines in the gloom
And shadows shudder close at hand.

Chorus
Sing, sing, our praises bring,
The dawn lights up the distant east,
Sing, sing our praises bring,
The sun will come in its glory.

2 No sound is heard from sleeping birds,
  And frost is white on the roads and grass;
  There are no signs of warmer times,
  No buds to show that winter's passed.
  Chorus

3 When darkest fears and thoughts appear,
  The clouds are grey and cheerless,
  When friends have gone, we're all alone,
  The day looks cold and lifeless.
  Chorus

Geoffrey Gardner

93

1 Morning sun, morning sun,
  Lights the day that's just begun,
  Helping everyone to see
  How beautiful the world can be.

2 Midday sun, midday sun,
  All the warmest light has come,
  Brightening our lives below,
  Helping all the plants to grow.

3 Setting sun, setting sun,
  When the day is nearly done,
  Moving all the light away,
  Till you rise another day.

4 Shining sun, shining sun,
  Bringing life to everyone,
  Helping all the world to see,
  You shine on us eternally.
  Jill Darby

94

1 (1) Make us worthy, Lord,
  (2) *Make us worthy, Lord.*
  (1) To serve our fellow men,
  (2) *To serve our fellow men.*
  (1) Make us worthy, Lord,
  (2) *Make us worthy, Lord.*
  (1) To serve our fellow men,
  (2) *To serve our fellow men.*
  (1) Throughout the world who live and die,
  (2) *Throughout the world who live and die,*
  (1) In poverty and hunger,
  (2) *In poverty and hunger,*
  (1) In poverty and hunger,
  (2) *In poverty and hunger.*

2 (1) Give them, through our hands,
  (2) *Give them, through our hands,*
  (1) This day, their daily bread,
  (2) *This day, their daily bread.*
  (1) Give them, through our hands,
  (2) *Give them, through our hands,*
  (1) This day, their daily bread,
  (2) *This day, their daily bread.*
  (1) And by our understanding love,
  (2) *And by our understanding love,*
  (1) Give peace and joy,
  (2) *Give peace and joy,*
  (1) Give peace and joy,
  (2) *Give peace and joy.*

Traditional

This is often known as 'Mother Teresa's Daily Prayer'. The song can be sung by two groups, indicated by (1) and (2). Group (2) echoes the tune and words sung by Group (1). Alternatively, it may be sung without the echoing phrases.

Short version

1 Make us worthy, Lord,
  To serve our fellow men;
  Make us worthy, Lord,
  To serve our fellow men,

Throughout the world who live and die,
In poverty and hunger,
In poverty and hunger.

2 Give them, through our hands,
This day, their daily bread;
Give them, through our hands,
This day, their daily bread,
And by our understanding love,
Give peace and joy,
Give peace and joy.

95 Rejoice in the Lord always
and again I say rejoice.
Rejoice in the Lord always
and again I say rejoice.
Rejoice, rejoice,
and again I say rejoice,
Rejoice, rejoice,
and again I say rejoice.

Traditional

This is based on Philippians 4:4. The song may be sung as a round.

96 1 A still small voice in the heart of the city,
A still small voice on the mountain,
Through the storms that are raging or the quiet
of the evening,
It can only be heard if you listen.

2 The voice of God in a place that is troubled,
The voice of God in the dawn,
Through the noise of the shouting,
Through the still sound of the sleeping,
It can only be heard if you listen.

3 Give time to hear, give us love to listen,
Give wisdom for understanding,
There's a still, small voice which to each one is
speaking,
If we only have the time to listen.

Jancis Harvey

97 'Tis the gift to be simple, 'tis the gift to be free,
'Tis the gift to come down where you ought to
be,
And when we find ourselves in the place just
right,
'Twill be in the valley of love and delight.

Chorus:
When true simplicity is gained,
To bow and to bend we shan't be ashamed;
To turn, turn will be our delight,
Till by turning, turning we come round right.

Traditional. A Shaker song. The melody of 'Lord
of the Dance' is based on this tune.

98 You shall go out with joy and be led forth with
peace,
And the mountains and the hills shall break
forth before you,
There'll be shouts of joy and the trees of the
fields
Shall clap, shall clap their hands.
And the trees of the field shall clap their
hands,
And the trees of the field shall clap their
hands,
And the trees of the field shall clap their
hands,
And you'll go out with joy.
                    Stuart Dauermann and Steffi Geiser Rubin

This is based on the words of Isaiah 55:12. The
song can be repeated, getting faster each time.

99

Chorus:
Love will never come to an end,
Love will never come to an end,
Three things will last:
Faith, hope and love,
But greatest of all is love,
Love, love, love.

1 Like an angel I may speak,
   Know the truths that others seek,
   Give my goods and life away,
   I am nothing without love.
   Chorus

2 I may seem a great success,
   Wisdom, wealth or charm possess,
   Yet whatever I achieve
   I am nothing without love.
   Chorus

3 Love is patient, love is kind.
   Love requires a truthful mind.
   Love will keep no score of wrongs.
   There is nothing love can't face.
   Chorus

4 Childish thoughts are put away,
   Partial knowledge has its day.
   Love with faith and hope endures,
   There is nothing conquers love.

Chorus:
Love will never come to an end,
Love will never come to an end,
Three things will last:
Faith, hope and love,
But greatest of all is love,
Love, love, love.
Love is forever,
For ever and ever, is love.
                    Patrick Appleford

This is based on words from 1 Corinthians 13.

100

1 I may speak in the tongues of angels
And foretell with a heavenly song;
Should it be that my love is lacking —
Then my voice is a sounding gong;

Chorus:
Three things last for ever,
They are faith, hope and love;
And the greatest of these is love,
And the greatest of these is love!

2 I may give all I have to neighbours,
And explore every mansion above
To possess all the jewels of wisdom —
I am nothing at all, without love;
Chorus

3 By my faith I may move the mountains,
And may stand for a cause to be won;
If I do not have love in doing —
Then I shall be the better by none;
Chorus

4 Now this loving is kind and generous,
And a wonderful, glorious sign
Of the limitless, deep, compassion
From the Power, supremely divine;
Chorus

Ronald Green

This is based on words from 1 Corinthians 13.

101

1 In the bustle of the city,
There is life, there is love;
In the birdsong of the country,
There is life, there is love;
Down the streets and down the lanes,
Through the wind and through the flames,
Where the human heart is beating,
Give your life, give your love.

2 Where the voices lift in laughter,
  There is life, there is love;
  Where the tears fall from the crying,
  There is life, there is love;
  During health and during pain,
  Through the sunshine, through the rain,
  Where the human heart is beating,
  Give your life, give your love.

3 See the families, see the lonely,
  There is life, there is love;
  With the sheltered, with the homeless,
  There is life, there is love;
  To the young and to the old,
  Through the warm and through the cold,
  Where the human heart is beating,
  Give your life, give your love.

4 In the factory and garden,
  There is life, there is love,
  For the worker and the jobless,
  There is life, there is love;
  To all men and to all women,
  Through their dying and their living,
  Where the human heart is beating,
  Give your life, give your love.

Geoffrey Gardner

102 1 You can't stop rain from falling down,
  Prevent the sun from shining,
  You can't stop spring from coming in,
  Or winter from resigning,
  Or still the waves or stay the winds,
  Or keep the day from dawning;
  You can't stop God from loving you,
  His love is new each morning.

2 You can't stop ice from being cold,
  You can't stop fire from burning,
  Or hold the tide that's going out,
  Delay its sure returning,

Or halt the progress of the years,
The flight of fame and fashion;
You can't stop God from loving you,
His nature is compassion.

3 You can't stop God from loving you,
Though you may have ignored him,
You can't stop God from loving you,
However you betray him;
From love like this no power on earth
The human heart can sever,
You can't stop God from loving you,
Not God, not now, nor ever.

John Gowans

103

Chorus:
I am planting my feet in the footsteps
That are there before me everyday.
Taking my journey one step at a time
The footsteps will guide me all the way.

1 The road of life lies before me,
And I know that's the way I must tread.
But I have the signs there to guide me,
And my path before is clear ahead.
Chorus

2 There are turnings that sometimes look
brighter,
And ways that seem better to me.
And people who'd stop me from travelling,
But I'll keep to the footsteps I see.
Chorus

3 It's easy somedays to feel weary,
And tire when the journey is long;
But streams always soothe and refresh me,
And footsteps ahead lead me on.
Chorus

Jancis Harvey

104

1 Time is a thing
   Like a bird on the wing,
   Coming or going away.
   Time is a thing
   Like a bird on the wing,
   Coming or going away.
   Coming or gone,
   You're travelling on,
   There's nowhere you can stay.
   Coming or gone,
   You're travelling on,
   You're always on the way.

2 Love is a thing
   Like a bird on the wing,
   Coming or going away.
   Love is a thing
   Like a bird on the wing,
   Coming or going away.
   Coming or gone,
   You're travelling on,
   There's nowhere you can stay.
   Coming or gone,
   You're travelling on,
   You're always on the way.

3 Hope is a thing
   Like a bird on the wing,
   Coming or going away.
   Hope is a thing
   Like a bird on the wing,
   Coming or going away.
   Coming or gone,
   You're travelling on,
   There's nowhere you can stay.
   Coming or gone,
   You're travelling on,
   You're always on the way.
                              Sydney Carter

105

1 God of the morning, at whose voice
The cheerful sun makes haste to rise,
And, like a giant, does rejoice
To run his journey through the skies.

Chorus:
On, on, the blazing sun,
Give again your living light,
On, on, till day is done,
Shine again and bring new life.

2 From distant places of the east
The circuit of his race begins,
And, without weariness or rest,
Around the world he flies and shines.
Chorus

3 Just like the sun, may we complete
The tasks we have to do this day,
With ready mind and active will
Move on, with hope along our way.
Chorus

Isaac Watts, with extra words by Geoffrey Gardner

106

1 It's a new day, there's hope,
It's a new day, there's scope,
To face a different challenge,
Discover there's no end
To new beginnings
To the new things we can do.

2 It's a new task, there's hope,
It's a new task, there's scope,
To face a different challenge,
Discover there's no end
To new beginnings,
To the new things we can do.

3 It's a new skill, there's hope,
It's a new skill, there's scope . . .

4 It's a new friend, there's hope,
It's a new friend, there's scope . . .

5 It's a new year, there's hope,
It's a new year, there's scope . . .

6 It's a new week, there's hope,
It's a new week, there's scope . . .

Geoffrey Gardner
Choose the verses most appropriate for your needs.

107

1 You've got to move when the spirit says move,
You've got to move when the spirit says move,
'Cos when the spirit says move,
You've got to move when the spirit,
Move when the spirit says move.

2 You've got to sing when the spirit says sing,
You've got to sing when the spirit says sing,
'Cos when the spirit says sing,
You've got to sing when the spirit,
Sing when the spirit says sing.

3 You've got to clap when the spirit says clap,
  You've got to clap when the spirit says clap,
  'Cos when the spirit says clap,
  You've got to clap when the spirit,
  Clap when the spirit says clap.

4 You've got to shout when the spirit says shout,
  You've got to shout when the spirit says shout,
  'Cos when the spirit says shout,
  You've got to shout when the spirit,
  Shout when the spirit says shout.

5 You've got to move when the spirit says move,
  You've got to move when the spirit says move,
  'Cos when the spirit says move,
  You've got to move when the spirit,
  Move when the spirit says move.

Traditional

108

1 The Lord, the Lord, the Lord is my shepherd.
  The Lord, the Lord, the Lord is my shepherd.
  The Lord, the Lord, the Lord is my shepherd.
  The Lord is my shepherd and I shall not want.

2 He makes me lie down in green, green
  pastures.
  He makes me lie down in green, green
  pastures.
  He makes me lie down in green, green
  pastures.
  The Lord is my shepherd and I shall not want.

3 He leads me beside the still, still waters.
  He leads me beside the still, still waters.
  He leads me beside the still, still waters.
  The Lord is my shepherd and I shall not want.

Traditional, based on Psalm 23

109

1 Thank you for the summer morning
  misting into heat;
  Thank you for the diamonds
  of dew beneath my feet;
  Thank you for the silver
  where a snail has wandered by;
  Oh, we praise the name
  of him who made
  the earth and sea and sky.

2 Thank you for the yellow fields
  of corn like waving hair;
  Thank you for the red surprise
  of poppies here and there;
  Thank you for the blue of
  an electric dragon-fly;
  Oh, we praise the name
  of him who made
  the earth and sea and sky.

3 Thank you for the splintered light
  among the brooding trees;
  Thank you for the leaves that rustle
  in a sudden breeze;
  Thank you for the branches
  and the fun of climbing high;
  Oh, we praise the name
  of him who made
  the earth and sea and sky.

4 Thank you for the evening
  as the light begins to fade,
  Clouds so red and purple
  that the setting sun has made;
  Thank you for the shadows
  as the owls come gliding by;
  Oh, we praise the name
  of him who made
  the earth and sea and sky.

Susan Sayers

110

1 Sing, people, sing,
  And follow in a ring,
  Praise to God for all we do,
  Marching, seeing, hearing, too;
  Sing, people, sing,
  Sing, people, sing.

2 March, come on, march,
  Beneath the springtime arch;
  Primroses a special sight,
  Cowslips make the garden bright,
  March, come on, march,
  March, come on, march.

3 March, come on, march,
  Beneath the summer arch;
  Roses in the hedges high,
  Honeysuckle climbing by,
  March, come on, march,
  March, come on, march,

4 March, come on, march,
  Beneath the autumn arch;
  Hazel nuts are turning brown,
  Chestnuts too are falling down;
  March, come on, march,
  March, come on, march.

5 Sing, people, sing,
  And follow in a ring,
  Praise to God for all we do,
  Marching, seeing, hearing, too;
  Sing, people, sing,
  Sing, people, sing.

Traditional

111

Chorus:
Round, round, round go the seasons,
Turn, turn, turn goes the time,
On, on, on go the days and nights.
The circle's a changing sign,
The circle's a changing sign.

1 Swallows nesting on the wall,
Swoop in the summer air,
Fly a thousand miles to warmer skies,
There will be more next year, we hope,
There will be more next year.
Chorus

2 Sticky buds on chestnut trees,
Burst into candle flowers,
Bronze and glistening conkers hit the ground,
There will be more next year, we hope,
There will be more next year.
Chorus

3 Toads and frogs make for their ponds,
Swim and lay their spawn.
Twist and wriggle worm-like, changing shape
There will be more next year, we hope,
There will be more next year.
Chorus

Geoffrey Gardner

112

1 Lay my white cloak on the ground,
   Spring isn't coming, spring isn't coming;
   Cold, cold snow falling all around,
   Spring isn't coming this year.
   Paint the trees with my silver frost,
   Spring isn't coming, spring isn't coming;
   Under ice the earth is lost,
   Spring isn't coming this year.

2 My cold wind will make you frown,
   Spring isn't coming, spring isn't coming;
   Blow the chimney pots all down!
   Spring isn't coming this year.
   Breath of ice and cloak of grey,
   Spring isn't coming, spring isn't coming;
   Rattle hailstones all the day,
   Spring isn't coming this year.

3 Hear sweet birdsong fill the air,
   Spring will be coming, spring will be coming;
   Sunshine smiling everywhere,
   Spring will be coming once more.
   Through the soil the flowers peep,
   Spring will be coming, spring will be coming;
   Earth is waking from her sleep,
   Spring will be coming once more.

Alison J. Carver

This is based on Oscar Wilde's story 'The selfish giant'.

113

Chorus:
To ev'rything, turn, turn, turn,
There is a season, turn, turn, turn,
And a time for ev'ry purpose under heaven.

1 A time to be born, a time to die;
   A time to plant, a time to reap;
   A time to kill, a time to heal;
   A time to laugh, a time to weep.
   Chorus

2 A time to build up, a time to break down;
  A time to dance, a time to mourn;
  A time of love, a time of hate;
  A time of war, a time of peace.
  Chorus

3 A time to lose, a time to gain;
  A time to tear, a time to mend;
  A time to love, a time to hate;
  A time for peace, I swear it's not too late.
  Chorus

Pete Seeger

This is based on the words of Ecclesiastes 3.

114

Chorus:
Flickering candles in the night;
Darkness turning into light.
Flickering candles in the night;
Darkness turning into light.

1 Gather round the winter fire,
  Stop the chill wind's blow;
  Watch the flame and feel the warmth,
  Hands and faces glow.
  Chorus

2 Cards and streamers on the walls,
  Brighten up the room;
  Decorations, coloured lamps,
  Drive away the gloom.
  Chorus

3 Tell a story from the past;
  Celebrate in song;
  Those who changed despair to hope,
  And defeated wrong.
  Chorus

Geoffrey Gardner

Suitable for Christmas, Hannukah and Diwali.

115

1 'Come in, my royal masters,
   I'm glad to have you stay.
   I welcome you, and ask you
   A question, if I may?
   Why have you come this distance
   From where your kingdoms are?
   Oh, tell me, noble sirs, why are you journeying
   so far?'

   'Baboushka, oh, Baboushka, we're following a
   star,
   Baboushka, oh, Baboushka, we're following a
   star.'

2 'The star's a mighty marvel,
   A truly glorious sight.
   But, lords, you must stay longer —
   Oh, won't you stay the night?
   Do tell me why you hurry —
   And here's another thing:
   I marvel at the meaning of the precious gifts
   you bring.'

   'Baboushka, oh, Baboushka, they're for a new-
   born king.
   Baboushka, oh, Baboushka, they're for a new-
   born king.'

3 'Some king, to have such treasure,
   A star to show his birth,
   And you to do him honour,
   The greatest ones of earth —
   And yet he is a baby,
   A tiny man is he?
   O royal ones, I wonder, then, if he will
   welcome me?'

   'Baboushka, oh, Baboushka, oh, why not
   come and see?
   Baboushka, oh, Baboushka, oh, why not come
   and see?'

Continued overleaf

4 'I will, my royal masters —
But not just now, I fear.
I'll follow on tomorrow
When I have finished here.
My home I must make tidy,
And sweep and polish, too,
And then some gifts I must prepare — I have
so much to do!'

'Baboushka, oh, Baboushka, we dare not wait
for you.
Baboushka, oh, Baboushka, we dare not wait
for you.'

5 At last I make the journey —
No star to lead me on.
Good people, can you tell me
The way the kings have gone?
Some shepherds tell of angels
But now there is no sound.
The stable, it is empty, and the baby Egypt-
bound.

'Baboushka, oh, Baboushka, we know where
he is found.
Baboushka, oh, Baboushka, we know where
he is found.'

6 Through all the years I seek him
I feel him very near
O people, do you know him?
Oh, tell me: Is he here?
In all the world I travel
But late I made my start.
Oh, tell me if you find him for I've searched in
every part.

'Baboushka, oh, Baboushka, we find him in
our heart.
Baboushka, oh, Baboushka, we find him in our
heart.'

Arthur Scholey

*This is based on the Russian story of Baboushka,
an old lady who, because she was too busy, mis-
sed the Christ Child in Bethlehem.*

16

1 There's a star in the east on Christmas morn,
Rise up, shepherd, and follow;
It'll lead to the place where the Saviour's born,
Rise up, shepherd, and follow.
    Leave your sheep, and leave your lambs,
    Rise up, shepherd, and follow,
    Leave your ewes and leave your rams,
    Rise up, shepherd, and follow.
    Follow, follow,
    Rise up, shepherd, and follow,
    Follow the star of Bethlehem,
    Rise up, shepherd, and follow.

2 If you take good heed to the angel's words,
Rise up, shephered, and follow,
You'll forget your flocks and forget your herds,
Rise up, shepherd, and follow.
    Leave your sheep, and leave your lambs,
    Rise up, shepherd, and follow,
    Leave your ewes and leave your rams,
    Rise up, shepherd, and follow.
    Follow, follow,
    Rise up, shepherd, and follow,
    Follow the star of Bethlehem,
    Rise up, shepherd, and follow.

Traditional

17

1 I want to see your baby boy,
But have no gift for you,
So, Mary, if you'll pardon me
There's one thing I can do:

Chorus:
I'll sing a song,
A special song,
Written for a king;
I bring a song,
A special song,
I bring a song to sing.

2 I've never heard of myrrh before,
I don't know where it's found.
I haven't any frankincense,
There's not much gold around:
Chorus

3 I have no words of good advice
To help him on his way,
But there is one thing I can do
Upon this special day:
Chorus

Elizabeth Bennett

118

1 When the winter day is dying
And the wind is blowing wild,
Listen for a lonely crying,
It may be the wandering Child.
Light a candle in your window
Let the night know that you care.
Light a candle in the window,
It may guide the Christ-Child there.

2 When at times you fear to follow
On the track that you must tread,
Friendly promises are hollow
For the tests that lie ahead —
Light a candle in your window
When your final hope is gone.
Light a candle in the window,
And the Child will lead you on.

3 When the world outside is waiting
But you can't give any more —
There's no end to war and hating
And you long to close the door —
Light a candle in your window
Let it shine beyond your pain.
Light a candle in the window,
And the Child will come again.
Arthur Scholey

119

1 The holly and the ivy,
When they are both full grown;
Of all the trees that are in the wood,
The holly bears the crown:

Chorus:
The rising of the sun,
And the running of the deer,
The playing of the merry organ,
Sweet singing in the choir.

2 The holly bears a blossom,
As white as the lily flower;
And Mary bore sweet Jesus Christ,
To be our sweet Saviour:
Chorus

3 The holly bears a berry,
As red as any blood;
And Mary bore sweet Jesus Christ
To do poor sinners good.
Chorus

4 The holly bears a prickle,
As sharp as any thorn,
And Mary bore sweet Jesus Christ
On Christmas Day in the morn:
Chorus

5 The holly bears a bark,
As bitter as any gall;
And Mary bore sweet Jesus Christ
For to redeem us all:
Chorus

6 The holly and the ivy,
When they are both full grown,
Of all the trees that are in the wood,
The holly bears the crown:
Chorus

Traditional

120

1 As I went riding by,
I saw a star in the sky;
I followed where it led —
And found a manger bed:

Chorus:
Little Jesus, show me the way of your love,
Little Jesus, show me the way of your love.

2 As I stood quietly still,
Some shepherds came from the hill;
Their eyes were bright with joy —
To find the baby boy:
Chorus

3 As I went riding back,
Some camels passed on the track;
Three kings had seen the star —
And hurried from afar:
Chorus

4 As I rode home to bed,
A thought came into my head:
God must love ev'ryone —
To give the world his son:
Chorus

Cecily Taylor

121

1 The Virgin Mary had a baby boy,
  The Virgin Mary had a baby boy,
  The Virgin Mary had a baby boy,
  And they say that his name was Jesus.

  Chorus:
  He came from the glory,
  He came from the glorious kingdom;
  He came from the glory,
  He came from the glorious kingdom.
  Oh, yes, believer!
  Oh, yes, believer!
  He came from glory,
  He came from the glorious kingdom.

2 The angels sang when the baby was born,
  The angels sang when the baby was born,
  The angels sang when the baby was born,
  And they say that his name was Jesus.
  Chorus

3 The shepherds ran to see the baby boy,
  The shepherds ran to see the baby boy,
  The shepherds ran to see the baby boy,
  And they say that his name was Jesus.
  Chorus

4 The wise men wondered where the baby was
  born,
  The wise men wondered where the baby was
  born,
  The wise men wondered where the baby was
  born,
  And they say that his name was Jesus.
  Chorus

Traditional

122

Christmas, Christmas, celebrate the time of
year.
Special days and special customs,
Special foods and special gifts.
Raise your voices in a greeting:
'Happy festival!' That's our wish.

Geoffrey Gardner

*This can be used for most popular festivals:
Easter, Diwali, Navratri, Holi, Hannukah, Sukkot, Passover, Eid, Baisakhi, etc. Substitute the
name of the appropriate festival. The song can be
sung several times, possibly becoming faster each
time.*

123

1 Mary had a baby, yes, Lord;
Mary had a baby, yes, my Lord;
Mary had a baby, yes, Lord;
The people came to worship him in
Bethlehem.

2 What did she name him? Yes, Lord . . .

3 She called him Jesus, yes, Lord . . .

4 Where was he born? Yes, Lord . . .

5 Born in a stable, yes, Lord . . .

6 Where did they lay him? Yes, Lord . . .

7 Laid him in a manger, yes, Lord . . .

Traditional

124

1 Riding out across the desert,
Travelling over sandy plains,
Comes a company of wise men,
Moving steadily along their way;
Leaving all their friends behind them,
Guided by the star so bright,
Now they've got to keep on going
Must not let the star get out of sight.

Chorus:
Riding through the desert,
Gently the wise men go,
Onwards to the king,
Who was promised long ago;
But they don't know where they're going to find
him,
There's many towns to search,
So they'll keep on following the star,
For it will lead them to his place of birth.

2 Wise men on their desert journey,
Travelled many miles so far,
Though they're getting tired and weary,
Town of Bethlehem is not too far:
How they long to worship Jesus
And honour him with royal gifts,
Hearts are full of joy and wonder,
As they're searching for the new born king.
Chorus

Peter Ratcliffe

125

Chorus:
Standing in the rain,
Knocking on the window,
Knocking on the window
On a Christmas day.
There he is again,
Knocking on the window,
Knocking on the window
In the same old way.

1 No use knocking on the window,
   There is nothing we can do, sir;
   All the beds are booked already,
   There is nothing left for you, sir!
   Chorus

2 No, we haven't got a manger,
   No, we haven't got a stable;
   Till you woke us with your knocking,
   We were sleeping like the dead, sir!
   Chorus

                                    Sydney Carter

126

Chorus
Little star stay with us,
Lighten the darkness;
Shine through this long night
And show us the way.

1 Little star shining,
   Tonight we are feeling
   You leading us home
   Though the journey is long.
   All down the centuries
   Travellers have seen you,
   And welcomed the warmth
   Of your silent night song.
   Chorus

2 Once you gave light
   To a dimly lit stable,
   And melted the chill,
   Where the new baby lay;
   Silently, gently,
   His sleeping you guarded,
   And stayed till the dawn
   Of another new day.
   Chorus
                          Jancis Harvey

127

1 Christmas time is here,
   Come and celebrate,
   Come and celebrate,
   Come and celebrate,
   Christmas time is here,
   Come and celebrate,
   Lift your voice in song.

2 Decorate your rooms,
   Come and celebrate . . .

3 Gather with your friends,
   Come and celebrate . . .

4 Meet to worship God,
   Come and celebrate . . .

5 Hear the tales of old,
   Come and celebrate . . .

6 Share the special food,
   Come and celebrate . . .

7 See the lighted lamps,
   Come and celebrate . . .
                Geoffrey Gardner

*'Christmas time is here', could be replaced by the
names of other festivals:*

Hinduism
Diwali is here
Navratri is here
Holi time is here

Judaism
Pesach time is here (*Passover*)
Rosh Hashanah's here (*The New Year*)
Purim time is here
Sukkot time is here
Hannukah is here

Sikhism
Baisakhi is here
The Guru's day is here (*for Guru Nanak's Birthday*)

Christianity
Advent time is here
Easter time is here
Whitsun time is here
Pentecost is here
Harvest time is here

Islam
Eid ul Fitr's here
The Prophet's day is here (*for the Birthday of the Prophet*).

128

1 Trotting, trotting through Jerusalem,
Jesus sitting on a donkey's back,
Children waving branches, singing,
'Happy is he that comes in the name of the Lord!'

2 Many people in Jerusalem
Thought he should have come on a mighty horse,
Lead his nation into battle —
'Happy is he that comes in the name of the Lord!'

3 Many people in Jerusalem
Were amazed to see such a quiet man
Trotting, trotting on a donkey,
'Happy is he that comes in the name of the Lord!'

4 Trotting, trotting through Jerusalem,
Jesus sitting on a donkey's back,
Let us all join in the singing,
'Happy is he that comes in the name of the Lord!'

Eric Reid

129

1 Jesus in the garden,
Sad and left alone,
Soldiers come to take him;
His friends have run for home.
    Jesus in the courtroom,
    Sad and left alone,
    People come to mock him
    In robe and crown of thorns.

2 Jesus on the hillside,
Sad and left alone,
In the silent darkness
He dies there on his own.
    Hiding in their home,
    Disciples lock the door,
    Frightened of the people;
    They go outside no more.

3 Disciples in the room
Feel sadness turn to joy,
Know there's work for them to do,
Throw open wide the door.
    Disciples meet the crowds
    To share their joy with them,
    Dance and sing to tell about
    The man from Nazareth,
    The man from Nazareth,
    The man from Nazareth,
(Nazareth)

John Tearnan

130

1 All in an Easter garden,
Before the break of day,
An angel came for Jesus,
And rolled the stone away.
And when his friends came seeking,
With myrrh and spices rare,
They found the angels at the door,
But Jesus was not there.

2 All in an Easter garden,
  Where water lilies bloom,
  The angels gave their message,
  Beside an empty tomb;
  'He is not here, but come and see
  The place where Jesus lay:
  The Lord of life is risen indeed,
  For this is Easter Day.'

Traditional

131

1 Now the green blade rises from the buried grain,
  Wheat that in the dark earth many days has lain:
  Love lives again, that with the dead has been:
  Love is come again like wheat that's springing green.

2 In the grave they laid him, love whom men had slain,
  Thinking that never he would wake again:
  Laid in the earth like grain that sleeps unseen:
  Love is come again like wheat that's springing green.

3 Forth he came at Easter, like the risen grain,
  He that for three days in the grave had lain:
  Live from the dead my risen Lord is seen:
  Love is come again like wheat that's springing green.

4 When our hearts are wintry, grieving or in pain,
  Your touch can call us back to life again:
  Fields of our heart that dead and bare have been:
  Love is come again like wheat that's springing green.

J. M. C. Crum (adapted by Geoffrey Gardner)

132

1 When from the sky, in the splendour of
summer,
Sunlight pours down over roof, over wood,
We sing of the kindness, extravagant kindness,
Of God who is Father and Lord of all good.

2 When all around us the glory of autumn
Colours the gardens, the fields and the hills,
We sing of the wonder, unspeakable wonder,
Of God who with joy both begins and fulfils.

3 When in the coldness and deadness of winter
Storms from the east with their bluster begin,
We sing of that morning, mysterious morning,
When Jesus was born in the barn of an inn.

4 When in the gladness and greenness of
springtime
Winter is over in life and in light,
We sing of that Easter, miraculous Easter,
That shattered the darkness and dread of the
night.

Alan T. Dale

133

Chorus
Lord of the harvest, Lord of the field,
Give thanks now to God in nature revealed.

1 Give thanks for the sun, the wind and the rain
And thanks for the crops that feed us again.
The corn safely cut is gathered inside
We thank you, oh Lord, that you can provide.
Chorus

2 The trees ripe with fruit stand proud in the sun,
We gather them now that summer is gone.
For yours is the wonder, yours is the power,
Yours is the glory of fruit and of flower.
Chorus

3 So in all our plenty, help us to·see,
The needs all around whatever they be.
With food for the body, strength for the soul,
It's healing and caring, making them whole.
Chorus

Jancis Harvey

134

1 I planted a seed
And now that seed is growing,
Oh, how that seed is growing
Out of all the ground of me!
I planted a seed,
But there's no way of knowing,
But there's no way of knowing,
Is it fruit or flower or weed?
There is no way of showing
'Till it blooms for all to see.

2 I planted a thought
And now that thought is taking,
Oh, how that thought is taking
Over all the mind of me!
I planted a thought,
And, love or hate, it's breaking,
And, love or hate, it's breaking
Out and never will be caught;
And love or hate it's making
Of the way you think of me.

3 I planted a word
And now that word is yelling,
Oh, how that word is yelling
Out of all the mouth of me!
I planted a word
And truth or lie it's telling,
And truth or lie it's telling
Just whenever it is heard.
Whatever it is spelling,
It will soon be clear to see.

4 I planted a deed
And now that deed is spreading,
Oh, how that deed is spreading
Far beyond the reach of me!
I planted a deed,
For good or bad it's heading,
For good or bad it's heading —
Oh who knows where it will lead?
Should I be glad, or dreading —
Here it comes straight back to me!

Arthur Scholey

135

1 Pears and apples, wheat and grapes,
Many textures, many shapes;
Falling leaves in golden drifts
Thank you, God, for harvest gifts.

2 Flashing shoals of silver fish,
Every colour you could wish;
Fishing boats, for you and me
Reap the harvest of the sea.

3 Deep beneath the ocean floor
Fuel and power have lain in store,
Brought to us through dangerous toil
Thank you, God, for gas and oil.

4 Coal black diamonds in the earth,
Ancient forests gave them birth;
Skill and labour now combine
Reaping harvests of the mine.

5 Earth and ocean, plant and beast,
Altogether make the feast;
All who long to share your grace
At your table have their place.

6 Loving Lord, we know you care;
May we all your goodness share;
Save us from all selfish greed,
Finding you in those in need.

Paul Booth

136

1 We thank you, Lord, for all we eat,
From farmers' fields and oceans deep;
We thank you too for those who toil
The long year round on sea and soil.

2 In stormy seas and shrieking gales,
In snow and ice and thunderous hail,
Men plough the waves and sow their nets;
They reap their harvest cold and wet.

3 From break of day till darkness falls,
In summer sun and winter squalls,
Our land is worked and tilled and sown,
'Till all hands ache and all backs groan.

4 We thank you too for those who drive
To bring our food where we can buy.
In shops and stores and market square,
So many work to help us there.

5 For those who live in distant lands
And work so hard in dust and sand;
Dear Lord, we pray that they will too
Have food enough to eat and grow.

Robert Smith

137

1 Michaelmas daisies purple in the border,
Big fat leeks all standing up in order,
Whiskered barley talking to the breeze,
Low hung boughs of laden apple trees,
Chugging engines ready for the reaping,
Pounds of chutney labelled for the keeping,
Giant marrows winning every prize,
Bubbling jars of elderberry wine;
It's harvest time, harvest time again,
Harvest time, thanks to sun and rain,
A time to take and a time to give,
A time to say that it's a joy to live.

2 Stocky-built trawlers landing with their catches,
Berries gathered, never mind the scratches,
Warm and hazy Indian summer days,
Swallows leaving for another place,
Fruits are bottled, others in the deep freeze,
Silken poppies blushing in the corn-fields,
'Don't bring muddy boots into the hall!',
Golden onions hanging on a wall;
It's harvest time, harvest time again,
Harvest time, thanks to sun and rain,
A time to take and a time to give,
A time to say that it's a joy to live
At harvest time.
Mellow, fruitful harvest time.

Estelle White

138

1 Now we sing a harvest song,
Clear and joyful, loud and strong,
Think of bread and think of meat,
Think of all we have to eat,
All God's gifts to us in love,
Earth and rain and sun above,
Thank you, God, for all you give,
Thank you, God, by whom we live.

2 Now we sing a sadder song,
Of injustice, hunger, wrong,
Those with not enough to eat,
Suffering every sort of need.
They've no home, no work, no pay.
Scraping through from day to day.
Do they thank you that they live?
Thank you, God, that we can give.

3 As we sing our harvest song,
Clear and joyful, loud and strong,
Help us, Father, now to see.
How to set those people free;
How to share the gifts you give
So that they may also live,
So the harvest song may sound
To your praise the earth around.

Alex Mitchell

139

1 Now the harvest is all gathered,
   Let us eat the Sharing Bread;
   'In our family, all together,
   As our custom is,' we said.
   And we pass the Bread among us,
   Thanking God that all are fed.

2 But there comes a gentle knocking,
   Just before we break the Bread,
   From our neighbours in the doorway:
   'Harvest failed for us,' they said.
   So we share the Bread among them,
   Thanking God that all are fed.

3 Soon we hear a growing murmur,
   As we eat the Sharing Bread,
   From the neighbours of our neighbours:
   'We are starving, friends,' it said.
   Then we stretch the Bread out further
   Thanking God that all are fed.

4 When the world begins to clamour,
   We cry, 'Take our Sharing Bread,
   Miracles we cannot offer!'
   'Oh, it happened once,' they said,
   'Thousands of us ate together
   Thanking God that all are fed.'

Arthur Scholey

140

(1) Lead me from death to life
(2) *Lead me from death to life,*
(1) From falsehood to truth.
(2) *From falsehood to truth.*

(1) Lead me from despair to hope
(2) *Lead me from despair to hope,*
(1) From fear to trust
(2) *From fear to trust.*

(1) Lead me from hate to love
(2) *Lead me from hate to love,*
(1) From war to peace
(2) *From war to peace.*

(1) Let peace fill our heart, our world
(2) *Let peace fill our heart, our world*
(1) Our universe
(2) *Our universe.*

Short version
Lead me from death to life,
From falsehood to truth.

Lead me from despair to hope,
From fear to trust.

Lead me from hate to love,
From war to peace.

Let peace fill our heart, our world
Our universe.

Adapted by Satish Kumar from 'The Upanishads'. In 1981 Mother Teresa urged everyone to use The Peace Prayer daily. The song can be sung by two groups, indicated by (1) and (2). Group (2) echoes the tune and words sung by Group (1).

141

Shalom, Shalom,
May peace be with you,
Throughout your days;
In all that you do,
May peace be with you,
Shalom, Shalom.
> *Traditional, adapted by Geoffrey Gardner*

'Shalom' is a Hebrew word meaning 'peace'. This song may be sung as a round.

142

1 I'm gonna lay down my sword and shield,
Down by the riverside,
Down by the riverside,
Down by the riverside,
I'm gonna lay down my sword and shield,
Down by the riverside,
Down by the riverside.

Chorus:
I ain't gonna study war no more,
I ain't gonna study war no more,
I ain't gonna study war no more;
I ain't gonna study war no more,
I ain't gonna study war no more,
I ain't gonna study war no more,

2 I'm gonna talk with the Prince of peace,
Down by the riverside,
Down by the riverside,
Down by the riverside,
I'm gonna talk with the Prince of peace,
Down by the riverside,
Down by the riverside.
Chorus

3 I'm gonna shake hands with everyone,
Down by the riverside,
Down by the riverside,
Down by the riverside,
I'm gonna shake hands with everyone,
Down by the riverside,
Down by the riverside.
Chorus

4 I'm gonna walk with my friends in peace,
Down by the riverside,
Down by the riverside,
Down by the riverside,
I'm gonna walk with my friends in peace,
Down by the riverside,
Down by the riverside.
Chorus

Traditional

43

1 I've got peace like a river,
  Peace like a river,
  I've got peace like a river in my soul;
  I've got peace like a river,
  Peace like a river,
  I've got peace like a river in my soul.

2 I've got love like a river,
  Love like a river,
  I've got love like a river in my soul;
  I've got love like a river,
  Love like a river,
  I've got love like a river in my soul.

3 I've got joy like a river,
  Joy like a river,
  I've got joy like a river in my soul;
  I've got joy like a river,
  Joy like a river,
  I've got joy like a river in my soul.

4 I've got hope like a river,
  Hope like a river,
  I've got hope like a river in my soul;
  I've got hope like a river,
  Hope like a river,
  I've got hope like a river in my soul.

Traditional

144

1 Peace is flowing like a river,
  Flowing out through you and me,
  Spreading out into the desert,
  Setting all the people free.

2 Love is flowing like a river,
  Flowing out through you and me,
  Spreading out into the desert,
  Setting all the people free.

3 Joy is flowing like a river,
   Flowing out through you and me,
   Spreading out into the desert,
   Setting all the people free.

4 Hope is flowing like a river,
   Flowing out through you and me,
   Spreading out into the desert,
   Setting all the people free.

Traditional

145

Chorus:
O let us spread the pollen of peace throughout the land;
Let us spread the pollen of peace throughout the land.
Let us spread the pollen of peace, and make all conflict cease,
Let us spread the pollen of peace throughout the land.

1 Jesus has sown the seeds of love;
   Jesus has launched the grey winged dove.
   Let us make the flower grow,
   And let the people know.
   That Jesus has sown the seeds of love.
   Chorus

2 All it needs is our love to make it grow;
   All it needs is our hopefulness to show;
   And tell those who are choked with fear
   That the prince of peace is here;
   All it needs is our love to make it grow.
   Chorus

Roger Courtney

This was written by Roger Courtney for the Corrymeela Community, which works to bring peace and reconciliation in Northern Ireland.

146

1 We ask that we live and we labour in peace, in peace;
Each one shall be our neighbour in peace, in peace;
Distrust and hatred will turn to love,
All the prisoners freed,
And our only war will be the one
Against all human need.

2 We work for the end of disunion in truth, in truth;
That all may be one communion in truth, in truth;
We choose the road of peace and prayer
Countless pilgrims trod,
So that Hindu, Muslim, Christian, Jew,
We all can worship one God.

3 We call to our friends and our brothers, unite, unite!
That all may live for others, unite, unite!
And so the nations will be as one,
One the flag unfurled,
One law, one faith, one hope, one truth,
One people and one world.

Donald Swann

147

1 Make me a channel of your peace.
Where there is hatred, let me bring your love;
Where there is injury, your pardon, Lord;
And where there's doubt, true faith in you:

Chorus:
O, Master, grant that I may never seek
So much to be consoled as to console;
To be understood as to understand;
To be loved, as to love with all my soul.

2 Make me a channel of your peace.
Where there's despair in life, let me bring
hope;
Where there is darkness, only light;
And where there's sadness, ever joy:
Chorus

3 Make me a channel of your peace.
It is in pardoning that we are pardoned,
In giving to all men that we receive,
And in dying that we're born to eternal life.

Sebastian Temple

This is based on 'The Prayer of St Francis'.

148

Let the world rejoice together, alleluia;
East and west, with north and south sing
alleluia.
Let the world rejoice together, alleluia;
East and west, with north and south sing
alleluia,
Lift your voices, all you people,
Share with others what you can,
Bringing care to those who need it,
Peace in every land,
Peace in every land.
Let the world rejoice together, alleluia,
East and west, with north and south sing
alleluia,
Let the world rejoice together,
alleluia,
East and west, with north and south sing
alleluia.

Geoffrey Gardner
The verse is repeated, getting faster each time.

149

And ev'ryone beneath the vine and the fig tree
Shall live in peace and have no fear (*twice*)
And into plough-shares turn their swords,
Nations shall learn war no more (*twice*)
And ev'ryone beneath the vine and the fig tree
Shall live in peace and have no fear (*twice*)

Traditional
*This is based on words from Micah 4:3. This song
may be sung as a round.*

Index

Page numbers (feint) and song numbers (**bold**).
Titles which are different from the first line appear in *italics*.

Acknowledgements

The copyright holders of melodies and words are given below. Acknowledgement is due to the following, whose permission is needed for reprinting the words of the hymns.

1 words from *The Children's Bells* © Oxford University Press on behalf of Eleanor Farjeon; **2** words © Christian Strover/Jubilate Hymns; **4** words © Mayhew-McCrimmon Limited; **5** words © M. Payton; **6** words © Michael Saward/Jubilate Hymns; **7** words © Curwen Edition; **9** words © T. Dudley-Smith; **10** words © Oxford University Press from *Enlarged Songs of Praise*; **12** words © P. Booth; **13** words © Stainer & Bell Limited from *The Song of Caedmon*; **14** words © Mayhew-McCrimmon Limited; **15** words © Salvationist Publishing and Supplies Limited by permission of the International Music Board of The Salvation Army; **16** words 1977 from *Christian Aid Songbook*; **17** words from *New Orbit* © 1969 Stainer & Bell Limited; **18** words by Alan Pinnock © 1970 High-Fye Music Limited, 8/9 Frith St, London W1. Used by permission. All rights reserved; **21** words © G. Marshall-Taylor/Jubilate Hymns; **22** words 1963 from *Green Print for Song*; **24** words © G. Marshall-Taylor/Jubilate Hymns; **25** words © 1965 Josef Weinberger Limited from *Twenty-seven 20th Century Hymns*; **26** words © G. Marshall-Taylor; **27** words © BBC; **28** words from *New Orbit*; **29** words © J. Harvey; **30** words © E. Bird; **31** words © G. Marshall-Taylor; **32** words 1971, 1975 Celebration Services (International) Limited, words adapted by G. Marshall-Taylor; **33** words 1973 Josef Weinberger from *Teach Me How To Look*; **39** words © 1965 Josef Weinberger Limited from *Twenty-seven 20th Century Hymns*; **42** words from *New Orbit* © 1969 Stainer & Bell Limited; **44** words from *English Hymnal*; **45** words by Valerie Collison © 1972 High-Fye Limited, 8/9 Frith St, London W1. Used by permission. All rights reserved; **47** words from *Riding a Tune*; **49** adaptation © G. Marshall-Taylor/Jubilate Hymns; **50** words by Jan Struther © Oxford University Press, words from *Songs of Praise*; **52** words by Jan Struther © Oxford University Press from *Enlarged Songs of Praise*; **53** words © Mayhew-McCrimmon Limited; **55** words © Musical Gospel Outreach on behalf of McClellan/Pac/Ryecroft © 1974 Thank You Music; **57** words © T. McGuinness; **58** words © 1960 Josef Weinberger Limited from *Thirty 20th Century Hymn Tunes*; **59** words © T. McGuinness; **60** words © H. Charlton; **61** words © Chappell & Company Limited assigned from Bradbury Wood Ltd 1972 for all countries in the world; **62** words by W. M. Charter-Piggott © Oxford University Press from *Enlarged Songs of Praise*; **63** words © Scripture Union; words adapted by G. Marshall-Taylor by permission from *Sing to God* Hymn no. 102 'Spirit of God, unseen as the wind'; **65** words 1965 from *New Life*; **66** words © John Oxenham by permission of John Oxenham and Anthony Sheil Associates Limited; **67** words © 1970 Durham Music Limited; **69** words 1967 reproduced with permission of Lorna Music Co. Limited; **70** words © Herald Music Service; **71** words © 1960 TRO Essex Music Limited; **72** words © Arthur Scholey; **73** words © 1987 Ann Conlon; **74** words © Ann Sutcliffe; **75** words reproduced by permission of Stainer & Bell Limited; **76** words reproduced by permission of Stainer & Bell Limited; **77** © Geoffrey Gardner; **81** © Arthur Scholey; **82** words reproduced by permission of Stainer & Bell Limited; **83** words © Geoffrey Gardner; **85** ©

© BBC 1978 and 1988
First published as *Come and Praise 1* in 1978 and *Come and Praise 2* in 1988
First published in this edition 1990
Reprinted 1990, 1991 (twice), 1992 (twice), 1993, 1994 (twice), 1995, 1996,1997 (twice) and 1998

Published by BBC Educational Publishing, BBC White City, 201 Wood Lane, London W12 7TS

Printed by Bell and Bain Ltd, Glasgow

ISBN 0 563 34580 2